Students against sweatshops

Students against sweatshops

Liza Featherstone

and United Students Against Sweatshops

VERSO

London • New York

First published by Verso 2002
© Liza Featherstone and United Students Against Sweatshops 2002
All rights reserved

The moral rights of the authors have been asserted.

Verso
UK: 6 Meard Street, London W1F 0EG
USA: 180 Varick Street, New York, NY 10014–4606

Verso is the imprint of New Left Books

ISBN 1–85984–302–6

British Library Cataloguing in Publication Data
A catalogue record for this book is available from the British Library

Library of Congress Cataloging-in-Publication Data
A catalog record for this book is available from the Library of Congress

Designed and typeset by Illuminati, Grosmont
Printed in the USA by R.R. Donnelley & Sons

Contents

Foreword

Walk onto a college campus in Anywhere, USA, and you'll find a similar scene. From late teens to old twenty-somethings, most are dressed in the hippest fashions of the times. Many wear sweatshirts, T-shirts, hats, coats, or socks emblazoned with their college logo. They don't care much about worker exploitation, environmental destruction, economic apartheid and human rights abuses. For most lackadaisical college students, life means: (a) getting your ass to class, (b) ensuring you have cool friends, and (c) making sure you don't run out of money.

That's why the young people I have met through United Students Against Sweatshops (USAS) are so amazing. They have an unusual passion for justice, found only in one out of every thousand college students. They give up the most characteristic quality of college life – the lackadaisical attitude – and trade it in for a conscience and an organizing manual.

Students Against Sweatshops gives us a glimpse into the world of USAS. It's not a simple one to understand. The devotion of the students, our unending quest for solidarity, and our dedication to self-awareness and education are exceptional qualities. The internal struggles – our disagreements with each other, the discontent with our progress, and the racial tensions, the class divisions, the gender battles, the issues over sexual orientation – must seem amazing to the average person. But they have made us a much better organization. I'm not into shameless self-promotion. But it is no small matter for young American citizens from so many different backgrounds to make common cause in helping to empower those with almost no power at all.

Neoliberalism hasn't delivered on its egalitarian promises. The gap in per capita income between the industrial and developed worlds tripled from 1960 to 1993. And by 1999, the wealth of the world's 475 billionaires was greater than the combined incomes of the poorest half of humanity. USASers realized this years ago, and decided to do something about it. For this, and for the gains we've made, we deserve the recognition this book gives us. But it's a recognition that comes with a cost: the cost is knowing that we were able to build this movement because of our privilege, and that the real heroes – the garment workers themselves – will never receive the kind of attention we have.

There are many people not mentioned in this book who dedicated part of their college lives to making USAS into a viable, national organization. We are indebted to everyone who has given their time.

Barbara Ehrenreich describes solidarity as "the old-fashioned word for the love between people who may never meet each other, but share a vision of justice and democracy and are willing to support each other in the struggle to achieve it." I've felt this solidarity as an organizer with USAS.

Molly McGrath

Why a student movement against sweatshops?

Fourteen-year-olds, from Bangladesh to the Mexican maquila, working fourteen-hour days in factories that reek of toxic fumes; young women supporting families on some twenty cents an hour; factory managers who forbid sick workers time off to go to the doctor; bosses in El Monte, California and elsewhere who have, quite literally, turned factories into prisons, forcibly detaining workers in sweatshops surrounded by barbed wire – more and more North Americans are familiar with such images, and the brutality of the garment industry has even made it to prime-time television. On a recent episode of *ER*, sweatshop workers were killed in a fire when factory owners failed to provide adequate emergency exits. Kathie Lee slave labor jokes are ubiquitous on late-night television. Indeed, the public is so disturbed by garment industry abuses that in a survey conducted by Marymount University, released during the 1999 Christmas holiday season, 86 percent of consumers said they would be willing to pay extra to ensure that their clothing wasn't made in sweatshops. In malls nationwide, it's no longer unusual to overhear shoppers in front of a Gap store debating whether to go inside. "I've heard they use sweatshop labor," one will say.

The sweatshop's new visibility is due, in large part, to the efforts of the North American anti-sweatshop movement, a movement now led by college students. Since 1997, students have been protesting the horrifying conditions in the collegiate apparel industry, demanding better wages and working conditions for the workers who make hats and sweatshirts bearing their school logos. Anti-sweatshop activists are the most powerful and visible progressive presence on campus since the South African divestment movement in the 1980s, and recently they have enjoyed some concrete successes.

This book provides a brief history of student anti-sweatshop activism, and of its primary organization, United Students Against Sweatshops (USAS), a loosely organized network of more than 180 North American campus groups. Founded only in 1998, USAS is wreaking havoc on the corporate campus and scaring the hell out of multinational corporations, some of whom, like Nike, know they cannot operate without the consent of the world's young consumers.

Students Against Sweatshops explores the movement's major successes and challenges, and its inextricable relationship to its setting – the corporate university – arguing that, paradoxically, USAS, like many other contemporary student groups, is a product of that corporate university. The book also examines USAS's origins in – and relationship to – the contemporary US labor movement and to feminism, as well as its more tenuous relationship to struggles for racial justice. Equally importantly, *Students Against Sweatshops* argues that USAS is inseparably linked to the youthful, worldwide anti-corporate movement now visible at any display of conspicuous capitalism, from the 2000 Olympics in Sydney to the 2002 European Union summit in Barcelona. It concludes by looking at the movement's current priorities and likely future direction, arguing that USAS is providing a model for transnational student/worker solidarity. At the same time, USAS is becoming a more broad-based organization, one that spurs students to take on labor abuses on their own campuses as well as in Indonesia.

Unlike this student movement, sweatshops themselves are nothing new; in fact, they have always been the foundation of the garment and needle-trade industries. This is partly because the softness of fabric and complexity of patterns don't allow for easy mechanization, which is the way many other industries keep production costs low. The term "sweatshop" is about a hundred years old, deriving from the concept of the "sweating system," a network of subcontracted shops which "sweated" profits out of workers through long hours, low pay based on a piece rate, and poor conditions. Today, although apparel companies and economists tend to reject the word as "emotional" and inflammatory, most other observers find it an all-too-accurate description of prevailing industry conditions, in which workers' earnings depend on production levels rather than the hours they work, and where they are subjected to heat, fumes, insults, sexual harassment, physical punishments, and below-subsistence wages.

With the decline of transportation and communication costs since the 1960s, garment manufacturers have increasingly elected to avoid the relatively high wages of US labor by moving most of their factories overseas, often to countries that offer workers little protection. The industry has also become more ruthlessly competitive, as increasingly fickle consumer tastes dictate quicker production cycles. In an attempt to keep clothing prices low enough to seduce American teenagers, manufacturers pay the Nicaraguan and Vietnamese teenagers who make the clothes less than a dollar a day. It is a brutal game, one whose rules young people worldwide – workers and consumers – are beginning passionately to reject.

Behind the Yale logo

Living conditions

Sonia is a garment worker who has sewn Yale T-shirts; in 1999, a delegation of USAS students went to El Salvador to see her, and to hear her story. Her house contained one light bulb, one stove burner, a mattress on the floor, and a few chairs. Her five-year-old daughter has chronic health problems, requiring expensive visits to dentists and eye doctors. Sonia also helps to support her mother, who lives nearby; as a fifty-year-old, her mother is not able to find factory work, so she takes in washing and ironing and cares for her granddaughter. Sonia became a union organizer because she was fed up with the abysmal wages and work conditions in her garment factory, Apple Tree, a Korean-owned maquila in the San Marcos Free Trade Zone.

Surviving on $30 per week

Sonia's food budget depends on whether she can get overtime work – she has little security from week to week. Usually she can buy rice, beans, sugar, salt, vegetables, and soup. Occasionally she can afford some chicken. She used to be able to get milk sometimes, when it was cheaper. She uses rainwater caught in a barrel for laundry and bathing, and pays for supposedly potable water for her daughter from a tank in her neighborhood. Often, the water comes out yellow and contaminated with garbage; Sonia boils all of the water, but it still sometimes makes them sick. She buys cheap or used clothing and shoes when she has money saved up. Sometimes she has to borrow money from high-interest-charging loan sharks just to buy basic necessities or medicine for her daughter.

Hours and wages

Sonia received the Salvadoran minimum wage, approximately $30, for working from 6:45 a.m. till 4 p.m. Sometimes, Sonia made as much as $50 in a week when she worked overtime: Monday-Friday: 4 p.m.–7 p.m. and Saturday, 7 a.m.–4 p.m. During high seasons, Sonia would also work full days on Sunday and would stay until 11 p.m. approximately three times per week. Sometimes, workers must stay late to make the production quota but do not receive the overtime pay they are legally due. If workers make mistakes, they must stay to fix them without receiving any overtime pay.

Health and safety hazards

The dangers in garment factories include: extreme heat, lack of fans and ventilation, no masks to protect lungs from the dirty air, and chemically treated fabric. Workers suffer from headaches, dizziness, repetitive strain disorders, throat problems, and rashes.

Workers in El Salvador have money deducted from their salaries to pay for social security clinics. Apple Tree, however, often refuses to give sick workers permission to go to these clinics and refuses to help workers get treatment for injuries caused by factory negligence.

Worker abuse

Apple Tree workers are constantly treated in a dehumanizing, abusive manner. Sonia reports that the supervisors swear, call the workers names like "pubic hair," and physically abuse them.

Workers are not allowed to talk, eat, or leave the production area.

Workers are only allowed one trip to the bathroom in the morning and one in the afternoon. There are too few bathrooms, and the bathrooms are disgustingly dirty. If workers spend "too long" in the bathroom, supervisors chastise them or even come in and hit them.

Women, the majority of garment workers, are particularly vulnerable. At Apple Tree, they must undergo forced pregnancy tests by company doctors (which the workers have to pay for) and sexual harassment from managers, including demands for sex.

Cheated out of severance pay

When Sonia was fired by Apple Tree, for union organizing, she was legally owed 1071.29 colones (about $130) for severance pay and overtime. Mr Kim at Apple Tree told her that he would give her only 400 colones (about $50). If she wanted more, he said, she could take Apple Tree to court, which she has done.

Sonia's expenses

Sonia's base pay is 538 colones per two weeks. With many hours overtime, she can make 700–800 colones. Sonia's expenses for two weeks break down, approximately, as follows (these do not include basics such as glasses and eye patches (for her daughter, who has chronic eye problems and needs constant dental work), clothing, shoes, and water.

Electricity	30
Dental drillings for daughter	25
Supermarket food for daughter while Sonia is working	250
Food for Sonia at factory (workers aren't allowed to bring in food)	150
Breakfast and dinner at home	100
Transportation costs (assuming a six-day working week)	96
School for her daughter	55
School supplies for daughter	5
Total (colones)	711

Jess Champagne

one

"They kick you in the teeth": anti-sweat activism, 1996–97

"They kick you in the teeth." Talk-show host Kathie Lee might have been wailing about the armed guards that intimidate and physically assault the young Honduran women who sew the clothes bearing her label. But, instead, Lee was in tears over her own treatment; anti-sweatshop crusader Charlie Kernaghan had been cruel and unfeeling enough to reveal that Honduran children worked fifteen hours a day in factories producing apparel bearing the celebrity's name.

The public was moved, but not by Lee's on-screen histrionics, attractively performed on her own show. Kernaghan became known as "the man who made Kathie Lee cry" in spring 1996, over a year before the onset of the student anti-sweatshop movement. Throughout the 1990s, labor, religious and other left groups – many responding to increasing militancy from the workers themselves – had been deploring the low wages and unpleasant conditions prevalent in garment factories throughout the global South, or what is optimistically known as "the developing world." Those activists were instrumental not only in bringing apparel industry abuses to students' attention, but in helping to launch the student movement.

Kernaghan, the fiery, charismatic director of the National Labor Committee (NLC), has been fighting sweatshops in Central America since 1990. He was one of the most influential of these early anti-sweatshop advocates, many of whom pioneered the media-savvy strategy of going after prominent brands or celebrities, especially those with particularly wholesome images, like Lee or the Walt Disney Company. But the NLC was not the only leader during this period. Immigrant women working in the US garment industry were organizing in the 1980s, through groups like New York City's Chinese Staff and Workers Association, La Mujer Obrera in Texas, and California's Asian Immigrant Women Advocates. In 1990, the year sweatshops became the NLC's signature crusade, Fuerza Unida, a group of laid-off Levi Strauss & Co. workers in San Antonio, Texas, launched a national boycott of the company, demanding a severance package and retraining, and carrying out hunger strikes and pickets.

Also in 1990, the Clean Clothes Campaign began in the Netherlands, a coalition of labor, consumer, religious, human rights, and feminist groups which has since spread to nine other Western European countries. In California, the Coalition to Eliminate Sweatshop Conditions attempted, unsuccessfully, throughout the early 1990s to pass anti-sweatshop legislation (it would eventually pass in 1999). In August 1995, a particularly horrifying garment sweatshop was discovered in El Monte, California, where seventy-two Thai immigrants were forced to labor behind razor wire, under the close watch of armed guards. The Coalition formed a single organization, Sweatshop Watch, to help the El Monte workers pressure the retailers who were buying from that factory. Working closely with the El Monte laborers – some of whom are now labor activists – Sweatshop Watch was able to help them collect $4 million in unpaid wages, overtime, and damages.

One of the campaigns that would prove most influential to the student movement was the anti-Nike campaign begun by Jeff Ballinger, former head of the AFL–CIO's Jakarta office, who founded Press for Change in 1998. After spending almost four years organizing workers in Indonesia, he returned to the United States in 1992 and began raising public awareness about Nike's dollar-a-day wages in that country. Ballinger's campaign drew widespread media attention, and groups like Global Exchange, the NLC, and the People of Faith Network began anti-Nike campaigns of their own. Nike's "branding" as a sweatshop employer had a profound influence on students, since so many schools have contracts with the sneaker giant.

The United Needle and Textile Workers Union (UNITE), too, was outspoken in decrying sweatshops, and, like the other groups mentioned here, successfully used the prominence of companies to call attention to their abuses, most notably in its mid 1990s Guess Jeans campaign. Such campaigns reflected, in part, new AFL–CIO president John Sweeney's emphasis on corporate campaigns. The AFL launched its "Corporate Affairs" Office in 1996 – a multi-pronged strategy for fighting multinational corporations and winning gains for unions. A corporate campaign entails not only attacking the company at home – picketing the shareholders' meeting, or a board member's house, for example – but exposing its wrongdoings elsewhere.

All these efforts drew press attention to the plight of sweatshop workers, and to the complicity of America's favorite brands in their immiseration. Many US high school students were horrified by the stories of faraway teenagers working in extreme heat for pennies an hour and, most saliently for many, deprived of high school education. Sweatshops, Abby Krasner, then a senior at Brattleboro (Vermont) High School, said in 1998, are "a student issue, because these workers are our age. If they lived here [in the US], they'd be in school." Through organizations ranging from the left–liberal International Student Activism Association to chapters of the National Honor Society, these early student activists – many of whom, Krasner included, would later become leaders in the college anti-sweat movement – wrote letters to companies and staged protests at their local Eddie Bauer and Gap outlets. In California, hundreds of high school and college students rallied against Guess Jeans, protests made hip by the endorsement of rock band Rage Against the Machine.

Young people were outraged on the workers' behalf, but they were also moved by a sense that their own desires were being manipulated, that the glamorous advertising aimed at youth markets was a cover-up meant to distract from corporate wrongdoings. "We had been told we needed to buy these clothes to be sexy, to be popular," says Pitzer College junior Evelyn Zepeda, who is active in United Students Against Sweatshops (USAS). Discovering the work conditions behind these desperately coveted labels, she says, "We felt used." This period's excessive materialism spawned a small backlash, and a dawning consciousness of the consumer's everyday complicity in systemic evils. "The system is completely dependent," observes Liana Molina, a USAS activist from Santa Clara University, "on us going out and spending money on all this crap!"

Some companies attempted to improve their images by drafting codes of conduct, in which they deplored child labor, forced labor, and other atrocities. Individual codes, however, led to little more than "self-monitoring." In 1996, the Clinton administration, along with a coalition of apparel companies, unions, and human rights groups, responded to activist pressure and consumer outrage by creating a unified code, and a monitoring body that purported to enforce it. That body, which was called the Fair Labor Association (FLA), was in fact so thoroughly controlled by manufacturers that it would stymie any efforts at real reform, but – vintage Clinton paternalism – it was intended to calm concerned consumers and persuade them that the problem was under control.

Meanwhile, the beginning of a new labor consciousness was emerging on US campuses, as graduate students organized unions, and many undergraduates were accepting internships with the AFL–CIO's Union Summer, the program that AFL president John Sweeney launched in

1996 to place college students in summer jobs with unions. In this climate, some students began to research and challenge their universities' connections to apparel companies.

They began to see that college students could play an important role in anti-sweatshop politics. Collegiate apparel is a $2.5 billion industry; Nike alone had multimillion dollar contracts with the University of Michigan, Duke University and the University of North Carolina (UNC), as well as smaller deals with around two hundred other schools. Students at UNC began raising questions about their school's deal with Nike, while students at the University of Wisconsin–Madison, a Reebok customer, began inquiring about conditions in Reebok's factories. When Reebok fought back, citing an oddly Orwellian "No Disparagement" clause in its UW contract, which apparently meant nobody at the school could criticize the company, students and faculty were enraged at the affront to academic freedom. They began a "Disparage Reebok" campaign that greatly embarrassed the company. Reebok, which normally holds itself up as a paragon of social responsibility, dropped the clause.

But the campus movement didn't begin in earnest until summer 1997, in UNITE's New York City offices. Ginny Coughlin, a newly hired UNITE organizer, asked UNITE's summer interns to research the connections between collegiate apparel and sweatshops for a possible campus campaign. That campaign, UNITE organizers reasoned, could complement the union's own anti-sweatshop efforts. Sensing that the FLA was helping manufacturers win the public relations battle, says Alan Howard, then assistant to the president of UNITE, "the union, to its credit, said, 'Here's a very important base that can help us deal with this offensive.'"

The interns researched their own schools, and found that administrators were doing next to nothing to ensure that clothing bearing their logos was made under half-decent conditions. One of those interns, Tico Almeida (see sidebar), then an undergraduate at Duke University, returned to school that fall. There he began a campaign to pressure the administration to pass a code of conduct requiring manufacturers of Duke apparel to maintain safe, independently monitored workplaces in which workers were free to organize. Fellow Duke students were enthusiastic and began lobbying administrators aggressively. They succeeded in getting Duke to pass the code, and the victory inspired students on other campuses to begin similar campaigns. UNITE had been discussing a campus campaign for about six months, recalls Ginny Coughlin, but Almeida "moved it in a way that no one had been capable of moving it. I was amazed."

In the spring of 1998, students founded United Students Against Sweatshops (USAS), a network of campus anti-sweatshop groups. It now has an office in Washington DC and several full-time staff members, and is funded by unions, foundations, and individual donors. But back on campus, most of these activists had become tortuously embroiled in meetings with administrators, negotiating the particulars of their codes of conduct. Duke students once again led the way. Occupying their president's office in spring 1999, they demanded that Duke president Nan Keohane add an even more crucial clause to her 1997 code: full disclosure of licensees' factory locations – so students and other researchers could investigate schools' sweatshop problems, and make contact with workers. After a sit-in that lasted thirty-one hours, Keohane gave in. A similar occupation won students full disclosure at Georgetown. In addition to disclosure, a sit-in at Wisconsin forced a commitment to a university-sponsored living wage study; Notre Dame and several other institutions have since followed suit with similar studies.

Shortly after the Madison sit-in, many administrators began joining the FLA, hoping to appease students by taking some action. Students, however, scorned that organization as a corporate whitewash. They weren't alone in this assessment: several unions and a religious group had resigned from the FLA in 1998, protesting that it was controlled by apparel companies, relied on "self-" or "voluntary" enforcement and set no standard for a living wage. The Clinton administration tried to get USAS on board with the FLA. Gene Sperling, the president's chief economic adviser, even offered to set up a monthly meeting with USAS members, but the students refused, not wanting to be used to legitimate a bogus organization. Student anger over the FLA inspired another round of sit-ins. Michigan students won full disclosure and a commitment to student input into the university's decision to join the FLA. UNC–Chapel Hill and University of Arizona students won full disclosure, a living wage provision in the school's code of conduct, and a commitment not to join the FLA (although the university did join the organization that summer, while the students were away).

With these successes behind it, USAS moved on to more complicated questions. Without a credible body to enforce them, students realized that codes of conduct were just pieces of paper. But that body had to be one that could build workers' power, rather than further erode it, as a corporate-controlled monitor might. Visiting factories and establishing relationships with workers throughout Central America and Asia, as well as working with union and living wage campaigns locally, students began to realize that unless workers have some measure of control over their own workplaces, even the nicest-sounding code of conduct is unlikely to do much good. USAS activists knew they needed to put this emerging spirit of student/labor solidarity into institutional practice. To this end, students, along with scholars, labor unions, and human rights groups around the globe, decided to found an organization that could serve as an alternative to the FLA, one that would be free of industry influence.

The new organization, the Worker Rights Consortium (WRC), would focus on investigating worker complaints rather than certifying specific companies or factories as "sweat-free." Developing a network of workers' rights groups in the global South, the WRC would aim to foster workers' own organizing efforts. Maria Roeper, a Haverford College student who took a year off in 1999–2000 to work for the WRC, explains why it isn't much like a conventional "monitoring" agency: "The idea of 'monitoring' is in some ways disempowering to workers, like 'We're watching you.' We're not doing that. We're saying, 'What do you need?'"

In order to get the WRC off the ground, however, students would need to persuade – or force – administrators to drop out of the powerful, Nike-backed FLA, and take a gamble on their fledgling organization.

"I'd never considered myself an activist"

When I was sixteen, I worked in a local grocery store in order to save money for college. After school and on weekends for about twenty hours a week, I stocked shelves and bagged groceries. Although the job could be monotonous and was far from lucrative, I never faced abusive or dangerous working conditions. I don't think I ever realized that in places like Nicaragua, people my age did.

When I enrolled at Duke University, I joined the Latino student association, and, like many of my peers, I enthusiastically spent countless hours living in Kzyzewski-Ville, the tent-city for students who want courtside seats at Duke basketball games. However, I came to labor activism a little more reluctantly. I signed up to spend the summer of 1997 in New York City teaching English to immigrant children, as I had done for several years in the Durham public schools. The professors who ran Duke's public interest internship program suggested instead that a placement with the Union of Needletrade, Industrial and Textile Employees (UNITE) – as part of the AFL–CIO's Union Summer program – would allow me to branch out into new service experiences. I disagreed.

I had never heard anything positive about labor unions. I was (and still am) strongly in favor of expanding international trade, so I had little interest in working for a protectionist organization. Yet, I agreed to at least research the option before rejecting it. I learned that most American unions are no longer against expanding trade, but rather are working with unions from around the world to push for trade accords that include and enforce the ILO's internationally recognized core labor standards. It also impressed me that UNITE funds a community center where the staff not only teach English but also help immigrants organize for better working conditions.

Intrigued by this combination of service and political organizing, I accepted a position at UNITE's Garment Workers' Justice Center in Manhattan. I met women and men who sewed for less than the US minimum wage, and who received no overtime compensation even though they were working well over 40-hour weeks. These immigrants were working hard but, unlike Horatio Alger's lucky bootblacks and chimney sweeps, they were not getting ahead. Nor were they giving up. That summer I joined immigrant workers in picket lines and protests, the first for me and for many of them. In addition to teaching English, I helped workers file complaints with the Department of Labor.

In one case that we worked on, a subcontractor that produced

sweaters exclusively for a New York City department store closed down overnight, leaving the workers without a month of pay. The workers were able to track the garments they had produced to the sales racks of that store, and they asked the management to take responsibility for the actions of its corrupt supplier. When the management refused, the workers enlisted the help of their local congresswoman, as well as of many local church leaders, and began picketing the store. Eventually, the store gave in to public pressure, paid the workers the back wages they were legally owed, and promised to be more careful in choosing suppliers. I came to understand that although the Justice Center and the Department of Labor can certainly do a lot to advance the cause of workers' rights, they will never be as effective as what workers can accomplish when they educate and organize themselves.

During my free time that summer, I worked with a few other university students – fellow UNITE interns – to research the collegiate apparel industry and to plan a campus anti-sweatshop campaign. The nine of us would meet to share our individual research and strategies for the campaign. We were also fortunate to have UNITE economists, researchers, international organizers, and activists to rely on for background information on sweatshops at home and abroad. (Some media would later use the union relationship as "proof" that the student anti-sweatshop movement had protectionist intentions, but a "Made in the USA" provision – whether in corporate or university codes of conduct – has never once been proposed by students.) As we reviewed all of the existing corporate codes of conduct, we noticed that not a single company included a provision for public disclosure of factory locations or independent monitoring reports. The conclusion was obvious: if we were to hold the manufacturers of our college merchandise accountable, we were going to have to force them to open themselves up to public scrutiny.

That fall I returned to the insulated and privileged life of a Duke student; yet I returned eager to persuade the University to use its leverage to push manufacturers to respect workers' rights in all of their factories, whether they be in New York, Central America, North Carolina, or China. I'd never considered myself to be an activist, but that fall I set out to try.

Tico Almeida

"A show of power"

At the beginning of bargaining, especially early on in our campaign, warmly greeting the administrators and asking how their week was going proved to be a good way to avoid an overly adversarial position (this took a couple of them aback at first). We surprised them by all wearing orange flowers one night, by presenting them with a Valentine's Day card to sweatshop workers for them to sign, and by inquiring about their vacations and talking casually one on one, with them when time allowed. In our most significant surprise tactic we filled the bargaining room with around twenty labor representatives from all over the state who were attending a conference near campus. After introducing everyone by name, union, and place, No Sweat! brought in a cake that celebrated full public disclosure. Soon, our administrators were mingling and eating cake with students and labor. It was a show of power by No Sweat! and it caught the administration completely off guard.

Micah Maidenberg

Is the movement "protectionist"?

The UNITE relationship has subjected USAS to some criticism that high school students, religious groups, and other non-union anti-sweatshop activists are less likely to face. Skeptics ranging from rabid free-trade evangelist Thomas Friedman to some Third World labor unionists have denounced UNITE's anti-sweatshop campaigns as protectionist, attempting to protect American jobs while jeopardizing those of workers in the Third World. The student movement, because of its relationship to UNITE, has endured this charge as well, from its earliest beginnings.

Students are sensitive to the "protectionism" charge; they go out of their way to emphasize that their own position is not anti-trade, and sometimes their image suffers from the unions' lack of clarity on this point. Sue Casey, a University of Pennsylvania USAS activist, recalls an uncomfortable moment when a UNITE official, presenting USAS with an award, thanked the student organization "for helping us in our struggle *against imports*." Since USAS goes out of its way not to take protectionist positions, Casey says, "that really stunk."

UNITE has engaged in such anti-import rhetoric, and indeed has sometimes campaigned against

lowering tariffs on imports. Defenders of this strategy argue, often persuasively, that a union is supposed to protect its own members' jobs. It has an obligation to protect the interests of its dues-paying constituents – who are, in the case of the garment workers that UNITE represents, among the poorest workers in the US labor force, and overwhelmingly black, Latina, and female. A union cannot always concern itself with the good of the entire planet, as students and religious groups are inclined to do, and at times the interests of workers in the US have conflicted with those of workers in the Third World. UNITE officials also point out that much of their "protectionism" has been intended to stop companies from roaming the world in search of non-unionized production lines, a practice that hurts all workers. But it has become clear to many labor activists over the past decade that protectionism in the garment industry, one of the most mobile forms of capital, is not going to end sweatshops, not in Los Angeles and not in Cambodia.

That is also increasingly clear to UNITE. The union's rhetoric – and perhaps its practice – may be changing. Increasingly, because protectionism has failed – the US continues to lose garment jobs to Asia despite tariffs, quotas, and labor standards – UNITE's recent international efforts have emphasized solidarity with overseas organizing. The student influence here shouldn't be underestimated. "We bring a more international perspective to the labor movement," says Jackie Bray, a University of Michigan sophomore active in USAS. "Students don't have the same responsibility to membership." UNITE's Ginny Coughlin agrees. "USAS has inspired us to think more globally," she said in summer 2001, a few weeks after the union had kicked off a new anti-sweatshop initiative, the Global Justice for Garment Workers Campaign, and announced a new worldwide coalition of labor unions, religious and human rights groups – including USAS. Union representatives from Canada, Mexico, Thailand, Nicaragua, Hong Kong, Guatemala, Honduras, and the Dominican Republic gathered in Manhattan's Judson Church, along with hundreds of UNITE members (mostly Chinese immigrant women who work in laundries and garment factories), USAS activists from all over the country, and community supporters. After labor leaders announced the beginning of the international campaign, the gathering, waving flags from around the world, assembled in the streets. Joined by several hundred more Chinese women bearing placards and parasols, the crowd marched down Broadway,

despite 100-degree weather, to protest at Eddie Bauer, Banana Republic, and Ann Taylor stores. The strategy, union officials explained, was to target a range of prominent retailers for the rest of the year, and see whether any of them improve workers' wages in New York City and abroad. The coalition planned to pick one particularly uncooperative company to target over the holiday season. The campaign had the strong backing of new UNITE president Bruce Raynor, who said at Judson Church, "This isn't about protectionism. It's about improving worldwide standards."

Many anti-sweatshop activists outside UNITE – including students and Third World labor activists – were immediately skeptical that any concrete strategy would emerge. Unfortunately, the new campaign quickly ran into some very bad luck: the global recession, and the devastating impact of September 11 on New York's garment industry. It is still moving ahead, but its future is uncertain, as the union has had to put most of its efforts into saving members' jobs. UNITE began a "Made in New York" campaign aimed at encouraging consumers to support Chinatown's garment district, a kind of local "protectionism." Under the circumstances, even the most ardent free-traders and internationalists would have a tough time criticizing it.

two

"I'd rather go naked": student protest and the worker rights consortium

"We have the university by the balls," said Nati Passow, a University of Pennsylvania junior, in a meeting with his fellow anti-sweatshop protesters. "Whatever way we twist them is going to hurt." The skinny, long-haired, and usually mild-mannered Passow was one of thirteen Penn students – the group later grew to forty – occupying the university president's office around the clock in early February 2000. The Penn students, along with hundreds of other members of USAS nationwide, were demanding that their university withdraw from the Fair Labor Association (FLA), and instead join the Worker Rights Consortium (WRC).

At first the administration met the students with barely polite condescension. In one meeting, President Judith Rodin was accompanied by U-Penn professor Larry Gross, an earring-wearing fifty-something well-known on campus for his left-wing views, who urged the protesters to have more faith in the administration. Gross mocked the sit-in strategy, claiming he'd "been there, done that." President Rodin assured them that a task force would review the problem by February 29, and there was no way she could speed up its decision. She admonished them to "respect the process."

Watching the Penn students negotiate with their university's president, it was clear they weren't buying her spin. Like the other USAS activists protesting on campuses all over the nation, they had sat through many similar meetings – all ending in blithe assurances and, eventually, broken promises. They knew there was no reason to trust that the administration would meet one more arbitrary deadline after missing so many others – so they stayed in the office. After eight days of torture by folk-singing, acoustic guitar, recorders, tambourines, and ringing cellphones, as well as a flurry of international news coverage, Judith Rodin met the protesters halfway by withdrawing from the FLA. (The institution joined the WRC the following school year.)

Penn's was just the first anti-sweatshop sit-in of the year. By mid April, students at the universities of Michigan, Wisconsin, Oregon, Iowa, and Kentucky, as well as SUNY–Albany, Tulane, Purdue, and Macalester, had followed suit. And the sit-in wasn't the protesters' only tactic: Purdue students held an eleven-day hunger strike. Other students chose less somber gestures of dissent. In late February the University of North Carolina's anti-sweatshop group, Students for Economic Justice, held a nude-optional party titled "I'd Rather Go Naked Than Wear Sweatshop Clothes." In late March, in an exuberant expression of the same principle, twelve Syracuse students biked across campus, 100 percent garment-free. The protests were a coordinated effort; members of USAS work closely with one another, a process made easier by the many listservs and websites that the students use to publicize actions, distribute information, and boost turnout. Like the disclosure protests of 1999, the 2000 sit-ins were extremely focused and coordinated: while students' specific demands varied from campus to campus, all demanded that administrators join the WRC.

The WRC's code of conduct is stricter than the FLA's, including a women's rights provision, more specific language on wages and free-dom of association, and less wiggle room on work hours. Though WRC members are not obligated to adopt the code, many have done so, and they are obligated to, at the very least, adopt a code of their own. The WRC's participating institutions must also mandate full public disclosure of licensees' factory locations. At the time of the Penn sit-in, the FLA did not hold university members to such a requirement. Although that has changed (there's no doubt that the competition from the WRC has greatly improved the FLA), the organization still does not require disclosure from its manufacturer membership. While neither organization requires member licensees to pay a living wage, the WRC has made a commitment to define "living wage" in its code after further study. That issue has been a contentious one. Shawn MacDonald, director of accreditation for the FLA, calls the WRC's call for study of the issue "ironic considering so many colleges faced criticism for joining FLA and were pressured to join WRC over this very issue." But the WRC's Maria Roeper points out that the "living wage" in a particular country should be determined by the people who live there – and without some "study" it would be impossible to know what the concept means to citizens of garment-producing countries.

The FLA's structure marginalizes universities – only one university representative can serve on its board at a time – and thus is less likely than the WRC to be substantially shaped by student activist pressure. Though all such differences have been important, the most salient one – and perhaps the one least likely to change – is that the FLA's membership includes manufacturers, and the WRC's does not.

Many universities that initially rebuffed the students' entreaties to join the WRC have since backed down, a testament to the skill and energy of the student organizers. The spring 2000 wave of sit-ins was deliberately timed to precede the WRC's early April founding conference. Before the Penn sit-in, only a handful of institutions, none of which had substantial apparel-licensing contracts, belonged to the new organization; by the end of that spring, nearly 50 had signed up. At the time of writing, in fall 2001, 90 institutions belong, fewer than the FLA's 161, but impressive for a new, grassroots organization with no corporate backing. (The WRC has professionalized significantly since its founding, now boasting several full-time Washington DC staff.)

The WRC's founding meeting, in April 2000 at New York City's Judson Church, was attended by students or administrators from forty schools. The night before the meeting, the entire ten-school University of California system joined the organization and sent a representative to New York for the event. Some institutions joined without any building takeovers, choosing to avert bad publicity through graceful capitulation. "A lot of them joined without a sit-in because they thought there would be a sit-in the next day," says the WRC's Maria Roeper.

Indeed, student activists did manage to put administrators on the defensive. On April 7 student anti-sweat protesters wearing duct tape over their mouths – to protest the fact that students have no say in campus decisions – met the University of Oregon president at the airport, frightening him so badly that he left the baggage claim and hid in the bathroom. Even more striking, that same day, was the sight of dozens of suited university administrators at the WRC conference scurrying to "organize" among themselves. Many were pressured into WRC membership and worry that they won't have as much influence as they'd like over the new monitoring organization. Administrators organized their own interest bloc, holding a separate meeting in Chicago that summer. "It's only natural that they should want to do that," said Roeper. "The student group [USAS] did have a lot of power."

The WRC strikes a blow, not only for global solidarity and workers' rights but also against the increasingly corporate nature of the university. Administrators were frightened by the organization's demanding code, but perhaps even more alarmed by the WRC's structure. By denying industry any role in its governance and vesting power instead in a board composed of administrators, students, and human rights scholars and activists, the WRC provides a nascent model for the kind of university decision-making the students would like to see: a process free of corporate influence. It is also a model in which, so far, student activists have set the terms of discussion. No wonder so many university administrators have resisted it so savagely – even, in several cases, permitting quite forceful police treatment of peaceful protesters. It is an implicit, ideological critique of the corporate university's priorities. The Universities of Wisconsin and Iowa sent in tear-gas-wielding cops to subdue USAS activists during the WRC sit-ins; the Madison police dragged away fifty-four students, in a move that George Becker, head of the United Steelworkers, amusingly denounced as "repressive... political correctness."

It is worth pausing to examine what is at stake, aside from administrators' ideological commitment to neoliberal development theory, which may vary depending on the individuals. USAS activists are part of a much larger global anti-corporate movement; this has placed them squarely at odds with the new corporate university, in which administrators brag about their industry "partnerships" and can sell the school's logo to Nike.

"That's just not the way this institution does things"

One late spring day, I was hanging out on Old Campus, one of the few open, grassy spaces at Yale, with a few of my fellow student activists, rejoicing at the near-end of finals. In the middle of this admissions-brochure idyll, Yale University president Richard C. Levin suddenly emerged. His head was bent slightly toward the ground, and he looked nervous, even afraid. It's possible that he had some important meeting to go to, a meeting that could intimidate even a Yale president. Personally, I think there's something about students having fun on Old Campus on a beautiful day that frightens or alienates Richard Levin.

I mention this moment because it reflects what I came to see as the relationship of the Yale University administration to its undergraduate students – one of distance, mistrust, and paternalistic autocracy. Over the course of the year that I worked on the anti-sweatshop campaign, I learned that, regardless of the merits of any particular point of view, there was only one opinion that would determine Yale's licensing policy: President Levin's. (Perhaps the trustees, many of whom run large corporations, influenced him behind the scenes. But there was so little transparency in the institution's decision-making that we'll never know.) Perhaps even more disturbingly, that crucial opinion was, until very late in the process, usually an unconsidered one.

Students Against Sweatshops at Yale (SAS) began in the early months of 1998, advocating standards for the production of clothing bearing the Yale logo. We called for a requirement that wages be high enough to support a worker and her family, and a means of enforcing such principles independently of manufacturer influence. We wanted Yale to use its name and its power to work toward better conditions in the apparel industry.

After a year of lip service and dawdling – missing its own deadline for the establishment of a code of conduct – the administration finally, in March 1999, made a change in its anti-sweatshop policy. Along with sixteen other institutions, Yale joined the Fair Labor Association (FLA), thus adopting its code, which did not at that time provide for full public disclosure or an effective wage standard. Moreover, the built-in inflexibility of the FLA, which required – and still requires – two-thirds of its apparel-industry members to approve any changes to its code of conduct, makes substantial improvements to the code highly unlikely. For these reasons, SAS wholeheartedly disapproved of the Yale administration's decision to join the FLA.

At around the same time, the Worker Rights Consortium was established, a body through which administrators and students could collectively formulate an effective anti-sweatshop policy, free from the influence of corporations. SAS proposed that the administration back up its claim that "we [were] all on the same side" by affiliating with the new organization. President Levin refused to do this. "We'll see how it develops," he said. When SAS asked Licensing Director Helen Kauder why Yale was not joining the WRC now, using its name and its influence to help the new organization become a viable solution, she replied, "That's just not the way this institution does things."

In February of 2000, after an entire year of discussion, the problems with the FLA had not been addressed, either by Yale or by the FLA. SAS asked the administration to join the WRC and leave the FLA by March 27. On March 4, 2000, SAS turned out five hundred people for a rally on Beinecke Plaza outside the president's office, the largest student anti-sweatshop rally ever. We followed this demonstration of our support on campus not with a building occupation or

increased demands, but with an attempt to compromise. SAS proposed to President Levin that Yale affiliate with the WRC, but conditionally remain in the FLA. We further suggested that the best way to make licensing policy would be not through rallies or arbitrary decisions by President Levin, but by forming a committee on the issue, made up of students, faculty members, and administrators. All members would be approved by both SAS and President Levin. SAS recommended that SAS and President Levin jointly establish criteria by which this committee would make decisions, and that the committee have final decision-making power on licensing policy.

In response, President Levin issued a four-page letter accompanied by eight pages of FLA-produced material, rejecting SAS's proposal and all of SAS's points as well. Disturbingly, he sent individual copies of these twelve pages to all 5,100 undergraduates on campus, clearly intending to cut off dialogue with SAS on these issues. By now *Yale's own licensing office* had come around and was internally advocating that Yale join the WRC. But not President Levin. He apparently believed in the autocratic system by which Yale policy was formulated by him, late, and without a critical analysis of the strengths and weaknesses of the different arguments in the debate. We issued a paper response, but realized that once again, our opinions were being brushed aside, and that this would continue indefinitely. And so we took action.

Beginning on April 3, for sixteen days, through frigid temperatures, gusty winds, and several snowstorms, we maintained a continuous, 24-hour presence on Beinecke Plaza, across from Woodbridge Hall, administrative hub of the university and home to the office of President Richard C. Levin. The occupation was a last resort, since Levin had already publicly threatened to have us arrested if we tried to occupy his office. SAS had been meeting with the administration for almost two years by then. Mostly we'd been meeting with Kauder, who had no decision-making authority. President Levin had spent, over the course of two years, perhaps five hours discussing licensing issues with SAS. He had a limited amount of time to deal with any particular issue – as he himself told us in his office in October 1999: "It's great that you're passionate about this, but I'm a university president." Of course, once we were living across from his office and, more importantly, publicly embarrassing his administration, he met with us more frequently. So, to sum up – students act nice, they get

five hours of Levin's time in two years; students engage in direct action, they get five hours of Levin's time in two weeks. Regardless, his refusal to delegate authority on the issue of university licensing had led to two years of bad policymaking, about 36,000 sheets of wasted paper – and a far more organized student movement. We failed to win any change in licensing policy through our occupation, but we did force Levin to hold an open forum on the issue in which any student could ask anything of him. He also committed to two more open forums in the 2000-2001 academic year.

Compared to other chapters of USAS, SAS at Yale was far less confrontational, both in the substance of its positions and in its means of dissent. Unlike most chapters, we were willing to concede to joint affiliation with the WRC and the FLA. We had meetings, leaflettings, and petitions, while other chapters had building occupations, arrests, and hunger strikes. I was proud of this contrast while I worked with SAS, because I believed and still believe that the policy questions at hand were more important than the power struggle over them – that the best solution would be reached through informed analysis and dialogue, not through a sit-in or an arbitrary decision by a university president. However, I can now see that our moderate approach failed. With President Levin running the ship, students who have any disagreement with the administration are forced to take direct action, because otherwise their views won't be considered. This was, in my view, the reason SAS's occupation received so much support on campus from other student organizations, from the student government to the Yale Equestrian Team and even some members of the Yale Political Union's Party of the Right — they had encountered similar high-handed and arbitrary treatment. The administration's approach to students is disturbing, especially considering Yale's tradition of producing CEOs, secretaries of state, and even presidents. Yale is training future leaders to believe that it is fruitless for the disempowered to try to participate in decision-making, or to oppose those in charge.

SAS's experience showed that there were serious problems with university policymaking. By that I mean that, whether President Levin was right, or whether SAS was right, the administration needed to be more accountable, more willing to hear from a range of constituents. I had hoped that, on their own, President Levin or the Yale Corporation (Yale's telling word for Board of Trustees) would recognize the limitations of an autocratic approach. I had hoped they would work with its students toward developing a better university as well as more ethical policy on Yale-licensed apparel. But that's just not the way this institution does things.

Saurav Sarkar

three

Student activists
versus the corporate university

Just about every aspect of collegiate life can be leased for corporate profit these days. Increasingly, universities outsource services they used to provide themselves; on campuses nationwide, big capital's irresistibly cartoonish logos are becoming as ubiquitous as backpacks. Barnes & Noble has taken over the university bookstores, and Starbucks has set up shop in the student union. It's not unusual for a university to lease the rights to its own brand name: the University of Michigan, for instance, recently signed a seven-year deal, in which Nike will outfit all of the school's varsity teams and pay $1.2 million annually for the rights to the school's much-coveted logo. Many schools make such deals with apparel companies: not only does the company then own the school logo but, in Nike's case, it gets to put its own Swoosh on the clothing, or on a big flashy sign over the stadium. Universities are run increasingly like private firms, and have ever more intimate relations with private industry.

Perhaps unhappily for school administrators, this transformation has coincided with a dramatic escalation, in both numbers and militancy, in student anti-corporate activism, of which USAS has been the most effective and visible organization. That groundswell owes much to the exuberant global anti-corporate – or, outside the US, anti-capitalist – movement, made visible by carnivalesque protests from

London 1999 to Porto Alegre, Quebec City and Genoa in 2001. In the US, that movement, which includes activists concerned about labor, the environment, Third World debt relief and numerous other issues, was immeasurably energized by and found expression in the historic November 1999 anti-World Trade Organization (WTO) mobilization, now referred to simply as "Seattle." Many students participated in "Seattle," but it was only a beginning. Since then, students from the University of California–Davis to the University of Vermont have held globalization teach-ins. They have urged their universities to boycott World Bank Bonds. They perform anti-WTO guerrilla theater. Many more helped shut down large portions of Washington DC in the April 2000 World Bank/International Monetary Fund protests.

With a *joie de vivre* that the American economic left has lacked since the days of Emma Goldman and John Reed, college students are harnessing their creativity, irony, and media savvy to launch a well-organized, thoughtful, and morally outraged resistance to corporate power. These activists, more than any student radicals in years, passionately denounce the wealth gap, as well as the lack of democratic accountability in a world dominated by corporations. While some attend traditionally political schools like Evergreen, Michigan, and Wisconsin, this activism does not revolve around the usual suspects: some of the most dramatic actions have taken place at campuses that have always been conservative, like the University of Pennsylvania, Virginia Commonwealth, and Johns Hopkins. This oppositional spirit is quite unlike the "don't trust anyone under 30" Oedipal crisis of baby-boomer protest. Many of the new activists have radical parents, even communist grandparents; rather than rebelling against the adults in their lives, they are following in their footsteps. Its regional diversity, too, will surprise observers of past US student protest – in addition to the Coasts, this student movement thrives in places ranging from the University of Tennessee to the University of North Dakota. Throughout 2000 and 2001, students nationwide were staging significant anti-corporate protests almost every week. It is neither too soon, nor too naively optimistic, to call it a movement.

Like other contemporary anticorporatists – those vandalizing and protesting under Golden Arches worldwide, or Charlie Kernaghan crusading against Kathie Lee and Disney – student anticorporate activists have expertly used big capital's catchy logos against it. Companies targeting a youth market are selling a brand as much as a particular product. The imagery surrounding such brands can be hypnotic, narcotic even, distracting us from the ugly social relations embedded in the manufacturing process. But as Naomi Klein observes in *No Logo: Taking Aim at the Brand Bullies*, companies trafficking in image are particularly vulnerable when those images are tarnished. Obscure information-technology companies can quietly outsource their data-entry work to Caribbean sweatshops, but companies like Gap are different: their prominence in consumers' hearts and minds makes it far easier for activists to publicize their wrongdoings. Nike has been a popular target among students, because even though exploitation pervades the industry, the sneaker behemoth's recognizable logo can help calls attention to abuses. Students at Ohio State, for instance, staged a "Smash the Swoosh" demo, gleefully destroying a papier mâché Nike logo like a piñata.

Just like the Swoosh, "we can think of the university itself as a brand, a logo, that students consume," said anti-sweat activist Todd Pugatch, then a student at UNC–Chapel Hill. Andrew Ross, chair of NYU's Department of American Studies and editor of the 1997 anthology *No Sweat*, agrees, pointing out that clothing bearing university names was stylish among young people even back in the 1980s, before the current romance with corporate logos. Before Fubu hats, trendy teenagers sported Notre Dame, Georgetown, or Harvard sweatshirts, whether or not they actually attended those schools. So it seems fitting

that in the global youth movement to expose the exploitation con-
cealed (as students often put it) "behind the label," a struggle over
university apparel should figure so prominently. Universities, especially
if they are academically prestigious, or have high-profile sports teams,
depend on image as much as Nike does, and the recognizability of the
University of Michigan's big yellow M, like that of McDonald's, can
backfire if the logo comes to symbolize exploitation and corporate
greed.

And indeed, much of students' anticorporate organizing has focused
on the reality of the university as a corporate actor. During one anti-
sweat occupation, for example, student activists at the University of
Oregon led a campus tour of sites that illustrated the institution's
numerous ties to corporations (one stop was the Knight Library, named
after Nike's president and CEO). A nationwide student group called
180/Movement for Democracy and Education, based at the University
of Wisconsin, articulated this problem and its connection to other
issues as early as 1999, leading teach-ins on how WTO policies affect
higher education.

Some of the student campaigns reveal the university as a stingy
service provider (those focusing on tuition increases, for example),
while others target the institution as an employer (fights over the wages
of university dining hall workers, graduate student organizing and, less
directly, apparel licenses). Many highlight the university's role as an
investor in the global economy – those pushing to make their school's
portfolios more socially responsible, for example. Others, like those
who protested in solidarity with the striking students in Mexico, have
strenuously objected to the worldwide privatization of public education.

A prominent feature of the corporate university is students' aliena-
tion and powerlessness; universities often treat them as anonymous
consumers, rather than as members of a community who deserve a say
in its policies. When administrators do that, they can expect student

customers to act like politicized consumer activists. "Campus democracy" is an increasingly common rallying cry (just as, at major off-campus protests, demonstrators chant "this is what democracy looks like"). Structural complaints about current campus plutocracy and autocracy abound: the powerlessness of the committees on which students and faculty serve, the influence of private-sector donors on school policy, the impossibility of getting a meeting with the college president. Whatever the issue, indignation over students' lack of power is pervasive. Like the idealists who wrote the Port Huron Statement, students are being politicized by disappointment: academia, they believe, is supposed to provide a space in which humane values at least compete with the bottom line. Many are shocked to find out that their administrators, many of whom now like to be called CEOs, think like businesspeople.

Some protesters have responded to the university's corporatization by rejecting it outright. In snowy January 2000, at Virginia Commonwealth University, twenty students slept outside the vice-president's office for two nights to protest the university's contract with McDonald's (the school promised the fast-food behemoth a twenty-year monopoly over the Student Commons). Simply saying "no" to corporate deals has its place; student refusal warns administrators that an institution's complex relationship to the global economy is closely watched and analyzed – a grenade ready to explode at any moment into messy and embarrassing dissent.

Yet even more often – and perhaps more shrewdly – student activists are making strategic use of the university's participation in the world economy. Universities' cozy ties to large companies are, paradoxically, a boon to the global economic justice movement because they bring corporatism into students' daily lives – and, perversely, lend students power as consumers in the "academic–industrial complex." Students are learning how to use that power, just as they did in the divestment campaigns of the 1980s, when students pressured their trustees to stop holding stock in companies that did business in South Africa. After all, if the university is a corporation, it's a unique one, in that a small number of young people can complicate its daily operations enormously. Though students are seldom given a legitimate role in making university policy, they still, as protesters, have far more leverage over the university than they have over any other kind of multinational corporation. When students understand the university's corporate ties, they can put formidable pressure on the institution to do the right – or at least the somewhat better – thing.

USAS activists have been at the forefront of this strategy, but they are not alone. Campus labor activists have targeted the bad labor practices of the behemoth management companies that run universities' janitorial, laundry, and dining hall services. Others have successfully pressured their administrations to boycott notorious union buster Sodexho–Marriott, a French company that provides campus dining services and is also the largest investor in US private prisons. This campaign, which began in April 2000, has inspired protests at Arizona State, University of Texas, Xavier, Florida State, SUNY–Binghamton, Fordham and elsewhere. It has killed Sodexho contracts at American University, SUNY–Albany, Maryland's Goucher College, Evergreen State, Virginia's James Madison University, and Oberlin, and forced the company to drop its holdings in Corrections Corporation of America, the largest private prison-management company in the US.

USAS activists – and the wider student movement they have so galvanized – are teaching themselves and their fellow students to question facts of social and economic life that they have been taught to take for granted all of their lives. "We are training an entire generation to think differently about [*pause*] capitalism," says Laurie Kimmington of Yale's Student Labor Action Committee. She glances at a reporter's notebook and giggles cheerfully. "Oops, maybe I shouldn't say that."

As Kimmington's good-natured hesitation makes clear, US students are far more readily anticorporate than anticapitalist. Yet, at times, anticorporatism seems too limiting a language. One student activist, interviewed shortly after Sodexho–Marriott's divestment from CCA, said she and her colleagues were still trying to kick the food service corporation off campus. Asked why – given the campaign's recent victory – she said, "It's a big corporation. We'd rather have some small local company make our food."

At such moments, one wonders whether anticorporatism is really about social justice, or simply an aesthetic objection to bigness. It has, among middle-class white people, become the dominant idiom of resistance in the US – even penetrating national electoral politics via Ralph Nader's Green presidential campaign – and in many ways it's a useful one. As the villains everyone loves to hate, corporate power and greed lend coherence to a global youth movement that's too often viewed as diffuse and lacking focus. Anticorporatism translates ad-mirably into union solidarity and, like "globalization," a term whose evasions journalist Doug Henwood soundly thrashes in *A New Economy?*, corporations provide a convenient euphemism for capital-ism, which few Americans want to talk about – after all, who wants to be taken for a glassy-eyed sectarian-newspaper pusher?

Students are well aware of the problem. "We need to develop a new rhetoric that connects sweatshops – *and* living wage *and* the right to organize – to the global economy," says the University of Michigan's Jackie Bray. Liana Molina of Santa Clara University, who doesn't shy away from the c-word, agrees: "I think our economic system determines everything!" But about USAS's somewhat vague ideology she has mixed feelings. "It's good to be ambiguous and inclusive," so as not to alienate more conservative, newer, or less politicized members, she says. "But

I also think a class analysis is needed. Then again, that gets shady, because people are like, 'Well, what are you *for*, socialism? What?'"

Outside of the United States, massive protests against the predations of capital are called anticapitalist, even by the press. But in this country, capitalism is generally treated as an irrevocable given, even by activists with no great fondness for it. Corporations, on the other hand, arouse tremendous resentment and ire. Even relatively conservative Americans can identify with Jimmy Stewart in *It's a Wonderful Life* defending the small business and small town way of life against the Bad Mr Potter, the corrupt embodiment of big $$. Or his modern-day analogues – Russell Crowe fighting big tobacco, or Julia Roberts and her breasts taking on the chemical companies.

As an enemy, the corporation would seem to have some unifying power; few people actually head companies, so in theory almost everyone could be an anticorporatist. And the movement has done a commendable job of expanding its analysis beyond institutions like the IMF/World Bank to a more expansive opposition to capital itself. But as many students realize, building a social movement to fight poverty may require a broader vision. Many people of color and poor people in the United States say that anticorporatism fails to describe adequately their experiences of everyday inequality and injustice. (This, of course, is part of the reason Nader's presidential campaign had more support among the upscale than among the poor.) Addressing USAS's summer 2000 national conference, Maria Cordera of the Third Eye Movement, a San Francisco Bay Area youth organization that fights police brutality and the prison industry, observed that poor people and people of color weren't so concerned about globalization. "That's not our bread and butter issue," she said. "We're worried about how we are going to feed our kids."

Complaints about "corporations" and "globalization" may not be adequate stand-ins for what old-fashioned radicals might call class struggle. For example, confronted with the problem of massive over-incarceration in the United States, student anticorporatists focus on those aspects of the prison industry that enrich private corporations, like private prisons or prison labor. Antisweat activists at California schools, for example, wishing to make common cause with antiprison activists, have been "redefining prisons as sweatshops," because some prisons lease inmate labor for corporate profit. This idea has been commendably effective in building multiracial coalitions between anticorporatists and young people fighting a racist criminal justice system. Yet the profiteering aspects of prisons are relatively peripheral, compared to the horror of prison itself, and to the injustice of sentencing policies. As Christian Parenti points out in his recent book *Lockdown America,* prison labor isn't as widespread as many activists claim, and, contrary to student and youth activist rhetoric, the lure of profits, whether through prison labor or privatization, does not motivate incarceration policy. Rather, Parenti argues, incarcerating large numbers of people is, "intentionally or otherwise, a way to manage rising inequality and surplus populations."

Another problem with anticorporatism is that it makes no demands on the state. Unlike European activists, who envision a clear role for the government in correcting injustice, US anticorporatists, especially young people, are wary of state power, and skeptical about government solutions. That skepticism is well-founded, and offers a valuable counter to a left-liberalism that has often been too dependent on a state that has, as Pierre Bourdieu observes in *Acts of Resistance*, largely abandoned its left-wing (social welfare, education) functions in favor of its right-wing ones (law enforcement, social control). Although we shouldn't hold our breath on this, the movement's anarchist tendencies may at some point help it to produce a coherent critique of the state's role in perpetuating inequality. They might also help the American left develop some brand of autonomous politics, an anarchosocialism that completely rejects nations, states, and national borders altogether.

But although that's a delightful long-term vision, it is, for USAS, becoming impossible to ignore the role of laissez-faire governments in perpetuating sweatshops. And the lives of poor and working-class people in the United States, at least in the short run, aren't likely to be radically improved by a movement that eschews state solutions. In the United States, in a time of ebbing government services and worsening economic equality, to simply repudiate – or, like most anti-corporate activists, completely ignore – the state is to write the majority of poor and working people right out of a movement.

The ending of what Bill Clinton called "welfare as we know it," for example, has wrought suffering on a par with sweatshop exploitation, and has only just begun to get any attention from the overwhelmingly white and middle-class US youth movement. Some USAS activists, beginning to move beyond anticorporatism, have been figuring out how to make common cause with welfare rights activists, helping the Kensington Welfare Rights Union, a welfare rights direct action group, fundraise for its Poor People's Conference in November 2000. In a similar confrontation with state negligence, throughout the summer of 2001, USAS activists, working with the Campaign for Labor Rights, visited twenty-five Mexican consulates to urge the Mexican government to enforce its own labor laws in a dispute at a garment factory in Puebla.

In addition, students fighting poverty in the United States must confront culprits more complicated – and closer to home – than corporate greed: class interests and an appalling collective indifference to suffering. This past spring, Dave Snyder, a Johns Hopkins student who helped organize a spring 2000 sit-in over campus laundry workers' wages, led a USAS delegation to Kensington, the desperately poor Philadelphia community in which the welfare rights group is based.

The residents "kept talking about the people who live in this nearby middle-class neighborhood, people who ignore them and shut them out," Snyder remembers. "I felt this rage against those middle-class people, trying to imagine what kind of horrible people they must be. Then we [the students] went to that neighborhood because someone's parents lived there, and I realized, this is my middle-class neighborhood; my parents would live here. I could live here."

Of course, such class inequality is what's wrong with America – and the world – and the corporation is just one of many instruments through which that inequality is maintained. In the same way, what's wrong with the university isn't the presence of Nike logos – unsightly though they may be – or even the fact of the institution's participation in the global economy. It's the meaning of these logos and deals – they signify that the institution is not run in the public interest, but to reap profits for the rich, and produce white-collar worker-cogs for the machine (or foot soldiers for the ruling class, depending on the prestige of the institution). As students are realizing, talk of "corporate control" becomes meaningless without some acknowledgement of class power. Indeed, if the public owned and democratically controlled corporations, and workers controlled their labor, the sight of a Nike logo would cause little distress.

"Smash the Swoosh!"

Pulling into Columbus, Ohio, at 1 a.m. on the morning of a big action, we might have expected to find the lead organizers trying to get some sleep. But the house was hopping when we got there – Alice Chen, Matt Teaman, Zakiyyah Jackson and other OSU radicals were bopping to music, joking around, painting huge banners ("OSU and Nike: Schools and Sweatshops Hand in Hand") and putting the finishing touches to a 10-foot-long papier mâché and chicken-wire Swoosh.

At the end of last semester a broad coalition of student groups at OSU came together for a sit-in in support of striking CWA workers that lasted twenty-eight days. Buoyed by the momentum from that sit-in, its organizers are starting an ambitious anti-sweatshop campaign in the fall aimed at getting OSU to join the Worker Rights Consortium. Revenue from OSU merchandise is among the highest of any school in the nation, and most OSU apparel is manufactured by Nike. Needless to say, the Nike Truth pilgrims were excited about the Columbus stop.

Early-afternoon rain cleared up just in time for our group of fifty or so students and local labor activists to set up a moving picket in front of Campus Expressions, a store which sells Nike-licensed OSU apparel. "Everybody wants to have a living wage. Everybody wants to be able to take care of themselves and their family. Everybody wants to retire and feel good, enjoy life. Breathe. Live. Eat. You know, the regular shit. We're not asking for nothing extra special," said second-year OSU graduate student Sheri Davis at the rally.

"Expose Nike! Smash the Swoosh!" we yelled as the afore-mentioned orange construction was torn apart at the end of the rally. From the hollow insides of the giant effigy spilled words describing Nike's business practices – "Poverty Wages," "Exploitation," and "Child Labor."

Chris McCallum

four

"Afraid of the movement": the backlash

"They must be afraid of the movement," says Jonathan "Doc" Bradley, a former US Army medic who is now a student activist at the University of Arkansas, "or they wouldn't be reacting this way." They" are the police, university administrators, economists, and corporate moguls who have been unsuccessfully attempting to crush students' persistent challenge to corporate power.

Indeed, USAS has faced backlash from its very own campuses – and not only from administrators. Disturbed by anti-sweatshop protesters' dominance over the campus discussion of trade issues, free-market economists – amusingly, a group whose ideology runs the world – have felt sufficiently marginalized to form a protest group of their own: the Academic Consortium on International Trade (ACIT). Founded by Columbia University economist Jagdish Bhagwati, its steering committee includes Robert Baldwin of Wisconsin, Alan Deardorff and Robert Stern of Michigan, Arvind Panagariya of Maryland, and T.N. Srinivasan of Yale. Of the six, Bhagwati is the most widely known to the general public, because he is a prolific writer of op-eds in newspapers, including the *New York Times* and the *Financial Times*. All six economists are widely published specialists in international trade, and all have consulted for governments around the world and for international institutions like the World Bank.

In summer 2000, the organization wrote a letter to university presidents, expressing concerns about recent concessions to students on apparel licensing issues. They claimed that raising wages imperils jobs – a common argument, but one that even Bhagwati concedes has yet to be borne out by the evidence (in fact, Bhagwati argued against putting it in the letter, but was overruled by the collective). In the letter the ACIT heads also rejected the FLA, thus placing themselves well to the right of Nike, which has worked closely with the FLA and unequivocally supports the organization. In addition to its drafters, 246 signatories endorsed the ACIT letter, including the Nobel laureate Robert Lucas of Chicago and Harvard's Jeffrey Sachs. Campuses with active anti-sweatshop campaigns, such as Michigan and Wisconsin, were heavily represented among the signers.

As it turned out, the ACIT letter has had little – perhaps no – discernible effect on university licensing policy, but the publicity it received inspired some progressive economists to act. One of them was Robert Pollin, a University of Massachusetts at Amherst economist and the co-author with Stephanie Luce of *The Living Wage: Building a Fair Economy* (New Press, 1998). Working on a paper that examines the ACIT letter's claims, he researched Mexican garment workers' wages – which are much higher than those in Asia, where most garment production takes place – and found that wages could easily be raised without any significant effect on the cost of the product. Together with James K. Galbraith of the University of Texas, Pollin has founded a group called Scholars Against Sweatshop Labor, and written an anti-ACIT letter that has been signed by several progressive luminaries, including Harvard professor Dani Rodrik, Boston University's Juliet Schor, and the University of Pennsylvania's Laurence Klein. The letter reads, in part:

> The current anti-sweatshop movement on college campuses can point to real achievements toward improving social protections worldwide: it

has increased awareness about the conditions facing sweatshop workers; and it has stimulated research and thinking as to the most effective ways US colleges and universities can contribute toward improving working conditions and living standards for these workers.

ACIT may have unwittingly helped the worldwide movement to improve labor standards – by bringing left and liberal economists into the conversation.

Intellectual backlash against the anti-sweatshop activists has not been limited to academia. Granted, the mainstream media has given USAS a great deal of favorable coverage, especially when compared to activists who don't attend "brand name" colleges. Yet even much of the coverage of USAS misses the issues, alternately praising and mocking student activists for their politeness, for doing homework during an occupation of the president's office, or for using cellphones to coordinate demonstrations. Some media trivialize the student protests, either treating them as rare epiphenomena that can't compare to the mayhem of the 1960s, or, paradoxically, as a too-frequent nuisance (in spring 2001, the *New York Times* noted that student protests had become yawningly predictable, a "rite of spring"). Yet such dismissals convey an intense anxiety. As the liberal business media (*Business Week*, *Financial Times*) keep – far more honestly – pointing out, there is a great deal of public dissatisfaction with the brutality of global capitalism, and it's not something those in charge can afford to ignore for very long.

Most telling are the articles devoted to defending unfair labor practices, because such coverage – in its eager, surreal feats of rationalization – reveals how deeply the anti-sweatshop movement worries corporate America's defenders. In September 2000, just months after anti-sweatshop protests had rocked campuses nationwide, Nicholas D. Kristof and Sheryl WuDunn, in an article in the *New York Times Magazine* titled "Two Cheers for Sweatshops," treated the issue as a cultural difference between East and West. The article leads with a description of a middle-aged Thai woman happily munching on beetles – "It was a hearty breakfast, if one didn't mind the odd antenna left sticking in one's teeth," the authors whimsically editorialize – and goes on to characterize sweatshops with similar never-the-twain-shall-meet relativism. "Nothing captures the difference in mind-set between East and West more than attitudes toward sweatshops," they argue, explaining that Westerners just don't understand that "their" campaign against sweatshops "risks harming the very people it is intended to help." Referring, rather incredibly, to Chinese sweatshops as a past-tense phenomenon rather than a brutal present-day reality, Kristof and WuDunn assure us that they "tended to generate the wealth to solve the problems they created." Sweatshops are a necessary stage toward prosperity for Asia, they conclude, neglecting to mention that wages and work conditions in China are still among the most abysmal in the world, unions are illegal, and efforts at reform so strenuously opposed that some industry monitors consider it "impossible" to do business there. In addition to such curious distortions, backlash pundits like Kristof and WuDunn neglect the fact that sweatshops don't allow any domestic capital accumulation and don't train workers for future, better work.

Of all the arbiters of the status quo, the apparel industry, of course, is the most terrified of USAS. Top officials of the FLA have toured campuses, trying to convince students of their organization's good intentions. For some time, Nike has been running a propaganda campaign to show how well its workers are treated compared to other workers in the Third World. This effort includes profiles of its workers on its website, nikebiz.com. The Nike workers freely choose to work in this factory and are using the opportunity to get ahead in some way – they are going to school at night, using this job as a means to a better life. Of course, these narratives are misleading; even the most passionate neoclassical economists admit that at best, workers see sweatshop employment, as Jagdish Bhagwati ambivalently explains, as "a ticket to slightly less impoverishment." Many workers do not have the educational opportunities – or even the means of survival – of those profiled on the site; indeed many Nike workers have complained to visiting USAS members that forced overtime prevents them from attending night school. And some of the Nike portrayals are racist, invoking images of simple "primitive" Third World folks who are easily satisfied with their humble lot in life (not unlike Kristof and WuDunn's happy beetle-eaters). One Nike worker, for instance, can't afford a television, but, according to Nike, "said her radio is all that she needed."

Nike's response to USAS has taken extremely hostile forms. In 1997, the company hired Vada Manager, a slick former Democratic Party operative, to run its PR, and his policy has been Clintonesque – indeed, he told *Newsweek*, it is modelled on the Clinton White House – to answer every attack, and to smear and intimidate opponents whenever possible. The glowing portraits of workers are accompanied by vicious attacks on USAS activists, especially Roselio Reyes, a Dominican student and former Nike worker. Of criticism from the anti-sweatshop movement, the amusingly named Manager has repeatedly told the news media, "Nike approaches this as it approaches everything – as competition. And we aim to win."

A week before the WRC's founding conference, Nike, which supports the FLA, canceled its contract with Brown University, objecting to the university's membership of the new organization. Nike has repeatedly denounced the WRC, calling it a "gotcha" monitoring system. "Nike is using Brown to threaten other schools," said Brown anti-sweat activist Nicholas Reville at the WRC conference. He was right, but Brown's chastisement failed to scare other institutions, and those that the company cared most about, economically and symbolically, were punished. Nike CEO Phil Knight, who had pledged $30 million to the University of Oregon for its sports stadium, indignantly withdrew the offer after the school announced its membership of the WRC, declaring himself outraged that the school would "insert itself into the global economy where I make my living." Perhaps most dramatically, Nike broke with the University of Michigan – by far its biggest collegiate contract – after the school joined the WRC. (Nike and UM have since made up, signing a seven-year deal.)

Such setbacks, although obstacles for the WRC – the University of Oregon has since backed out of the organization, inspiring Knight to renew his earlier commitment to his alma mater – have also served to rally sympathy for the anti-sweatshop movement. Even more importantly, the attacks show the WRC's power; clearly industry is truly threatened by the notion of a monitoring organization that it does not control – especially one that bears the stamp of legitimacy that a university's membership conveys.

USAS has made spirited use of Nike's assaults. Just as the academic backlash has inspired greater intellectual vigor in the movement, Nike's intransigence has prompted some of USAS's most creative activism. An excellent example was the organization's "Behind the Label" tour of summer 2000. After Nike's repeated attacks on the WRC, ten students, travelling by RV, made a two-week, eleven-city "Behind the Label" road trip. Accompanied by fired Dominican garment worker Roselio Reyes, now a student himself, they visited Niketown stores from New York City to Chicago to Las Vegas and finally Eugene, Oregon. The tour was launched to protest Nike's refusal to cooperate with attempts to improve work conditions in its factories, and the company's heavy-handed attempts to quash dissent on campus. They picketed outside, often with local unionists; and inside they attempted banner drops and other disruptions (see sidebar for a first-person account of this tour).

Throughout the trip, Nike personnel – including, at points, Vada Manager himself – followed the students, showing up at the store and even, creepily, greeting them by name. (Tipped off by school administrators and paid student spies, Nike also read web materials advertising the tour and knew who the activists were.) Students and unionists were met by police, teams of security guards, and often violence; one UNITE organizer got his rib broken by a New York Niketown thug.

But even Nike, an apparel industry giant, must now at least pretend to engage the criticisms of USAS and other labor groups. It has more at stake in the campus anti-sweatshop battle than any other company; it stands to lose not only multimillion-dollar apparel contracts, but the branding embedded in those deals: uniforms and even stadiums at most top sports schools bear its Swoosh. Each element of Nike's dogged PR campaign, and each new attack on the WRC, serves as further acknowledgement that anti-sweatshop protesters are beginning to set the terms of this global struggle. Throughout the first half of 2001, Nike made major concessions in response to student pressure on behalf of striking Mexican workers (see Chapter 8), and released a report on its Indonesian factories that confirmed almost everything that activists have been saying about them for the past decade.

Many bourgeois observers are beginning to admit that USAS and the rest of the global anti-corporate movement are a force to be reckoned with. Even USAS opponent Jagdish Bhagwati, talking about the new generation of activists, is strangely awestruck. "The kids really, when you see them, they are fierce," he marvels. "They're so fierce – they're carrying these placards, and they're all DOWN WITH CORPORATIONS! I'm putting the kids on the cover of my next book."

Truth tour diary

Day 1: August 3, 2000
New York City

It's not clear whether the Niketown in Manhattan hired extra security guards especially for today, but we know that several protesters and a cameraman, Jon Harris, were attacked violently by security guards when they tried to drop "Nike: Just Don't Do it" and "Stop Nike Sweatshops" banners from balconies inside the store. The store was taken over by eighty or ninety protestors, including supporters from UNITE, NYPIRG, and area students.

"All we are trying to do is tell the truth about Nike," said pilgrimage member Carrie Brunk, "and Nike responded with violence, just like they do in a much more frightening and threatening manner with their workers when they speak up about their rights and try to organize." "You've all seen Nike's new ads about the athletes who wear Nike clothes. Nike says that they deserve more love," SUNY–Cortland senior Marjona Jones said to the crowd during a rally outside the store after the banner drops. "But what about the workers who make the clothes? They deserve the same respect!" Before we got out of the city, we made one more stop. In the last few months, Kate Spade – a ladies' handbag manufacturer

whose products sell for $300–400 – fired every worker who signed a union card to be represented by UNITE Local 23–25: thirty-five workers in all. Truth Tour members stopped to lend support to the workers who demonstrated outside the Manhattan store today. The workers demanded to be reinstated and that the union be respected.

Day 7: August 9
Chicago, Illinois

This morning, Roselio and Jonathan (as a translator) were guests on the Mancow Muller's Madhouse Morning Show. Mancow is a controversial radio personality who has a morning radio show that boasts a lot of listeners, kind of like Howard Stern. To give you an idea of what it was like, one of the show segments that morning featured a camel-toed girl and welcomed callers to suggest something that could fit between her toes.

Roselio Reyes has his own radio show in the Dominican Republic, so he's very comfortable on the radio. He spoke about the physical conditions in the Nike sweatshop he worked in and about all the obstacles facing workers in the Free Trade Zones. Mancow is very anti-corporate and anti-big government, and he was appalled at what Roselio and Jonathan had to say. After a few minutes of interview, he aired a mock commercial for a product called Sweatshop Sweats. The enthusiastic couple endorsing the clothes talked about how little the workers who made them are paid, and the awful conditions they suffer.

At the end of the segment, Mancow did as Jonathan suggested and called up 1–800–EGG–NIKE, Nike's customer service line. When he got an operator he told them who he was, that they were on the air, and had a former Nike worker who would like to speak with Phil Knight, Nike CEO, about the conditions in Nike factories.

He never got Phil Knight on the phone, but the segment was successful in getting us all riled up about the afternoon action. About ten minutes after the show was over, we were painting banners on the sidewalk outside Granny Marjorie's (Truth Tour Pilgrim Marjona Jones's grandmother) house and a Department of Sanitation truck pulled up. The two guys inside asked us what we were going to do with the banners, because they just heard on the radio that some people were protesting at Niketown today. We told them that maybe we'd go check it out.

We were all very nervous about the Niketown action in Chicago. We knew that the Chicago police would be involved because Nike had called them. We knew that we had a lot

of support from UNITE union members in Chicago and Chicago students.

About eight Truth Pilgrims went inside the store and rallied and dropped banners that said "Say NO to Nike Sweatshops." They whistled and chanted and were kicked out of the store. We rallied outside on the sidewalk, but the whole thing was disrupted when a group of six or seven men bullied their way through the rally, with Jonathan in the middle. The people who arrested him were in Niketown uniforms, not police uniforms, and they had no badges visible.

Jonathan was put in a police van waiting by the curb. Chicago cops were everywhere. As soon as we saw what was going on, the protesters surrounded the police van and chanted "Let Him Go! Let Him Go!" We took out extra banners and stretched them across the front of the vehicle. Our UNITE Chicago contacts have some rapport with the police, so we agreed to get out of the way of the van because the police said they would negotiate. As soon as it could, the van pulled away and Jonathan was whisked to the 18th District jail, a few blocks away.

The remaining Truth Pilgrims led a march to the jail, demanded to know why Jonathan was arrested by Niketown security guards and why

he had not been warned before he was arrested, since all he was doing was videotaping. He was verbally abused but cooperated completely with authorities. "This shows Nike's willingness to go to any length – even violence – to keep their sweatshops secret," Jonathan said.

Down at the district jail, he sat locked in an interrogation room for an hour and a half, without being told why he had been arrested. We believe that in that interval the police went back to Niketown,

found a security guard who was willing to sign a complaint against Jonathan, saying that he asked him to leave and that he refused, which is not true. The security guard who signed the complaint just happened to be an off-duty Chicago police officer. Jonathan was charged with criminal trespass on property (the charge was eventually dropped).

The Truth Pilgrims sat outside the jail until 12:30 a.m., when they let Jonathan out. They kept the video-tape from his camera, which contains evidence that the complaint that was filed was completely false. They also kept his still camera. He got out on $100 bail.

Days 8 and 9: August 10 and 11
Chicago, Denver, Las Vegas

When I started this trip I figured we were fighting Nike. But now I think we're fighting Nike and the cops, because apparently the police just do whatever Nike tells them to.

Take today for instance: we had planned on doing an action at Niketown in Denver, but because we left Chicago late since Jonathan got arrested, we couldn't do things as planned. We did, however, stop at Kinko's in Denver to take care of some logistical things. Kinko's isn't far from where the Niketown is, so we decided to get some sandwiches and walk down there to eat lunch. There were about thirty cops down there waiting for us, who went into a flurry of activity when we got near. We were videotaped while eating by Niketown, surrounded by Denver police on motorcycles, bikes, and cars. There were plain-clothes police observing us. We were trailed by two cops on motorcycles as we walked back to the RV after lunch, and the same two cops rode behind the RV as we left Denver.

What's happening is that Nike is making it more and more obvious that they are willing to do anything

to silence us for trying to expose the truth about them.

Day 10: August 12
Las Vegas

The plan was to trickle in singly or in pairs, and then on a whistle signal one team would drop a banner from the second-floor balcony and others would chant and shout. We expected to be escorted out quickly by mall security. My partner and I, as unassuming as possible, wove our way through the crowded Caesar's Palace casino and the Forum Shops mall. At the door to Niketown we were met by two men, one of whom said, "Hi Chris. Hi Emily. You're not allowed in the store today." Well, that's nice, I thought. They've had ten days' worth of surveillance pictures to learn our names, not to mention the website. Emily and I watched as a young man next to us waltzed right into the store without a problem. The other Truth Pilgrims received a similar greeting.

Niketown security and mall security, some uniformed and some not, crawled all over the place, taking our pictures and videotaping us. A plain-clothes man followed Emily and me to the bathroom and around the mall a little after we tried to get into the store.

"They're making us feel like criminals for doing the right thing,"

Marjona said today in the RV after the action. We're even fairly certain that there were two motorcyclists, dressed like real Harley Davidson types, who were following us for hours after we left Denver. They ended up eerily at every single rest stop that we did and once asked me curiously what we were up to and where we were headed. That was after the police escort that was behind us in the city dropped off at city limits, which was after cops and security guards took our pictures and stood around and watched us eat lunch outside the Denver Niketown.

If nothing else, their surveillance has boosted our levels of self-importance. "We've got our own dude!" Emily said in the mall today when we realized that someone was tailing us. By the way, that dude will never end up in the FBI or anything, because he was so bad at tailing us. While I was waiting for Emily outside the bathroom, I noticed him watching me from behind a pole, for God's sake. I mean that's got to be the first thing they teach you about following someone – don't watch them from behind poles.

We reconvened in front of the Caesar's Palace Niketown. In a symbolic gesture of Nike's aggressive actions to silence us, we placed the bright orange stickers with our website (www.behindthelabel.org) over our mouths and knelt in front of the store with our hands crossed at our wrists. We attracted lots of puzzled gazes from shoppers – but Niketown got the idea.

Chris McCallum

five

"It's just like SDS!"
USAS and participatory democracy

Only a few of the USAS activists resemble – either in appearance or in tactics – the hooded anarchist kids from Eugene, Oregon, who famously threw rocks through Starbucks' windows in Seattle in November 1999. Many look as if they shop at the Gap (and some of them do). University of Oregon student activists, for example, don't have much in common with the marauding hooded Eugene residents who were such a controversial presence in Seattle and put the languidly countercultural college town on the national radar for the first time in thirty years. Agatha Schmaedick, a University of Oregon anti-sweatshop activist, laughs at the comparison. "It's ironic because people associate us with [the Black Bloc anarchists], but those anarchists think we're totally reformist!"

Yet the movement does have an anti-hierarchical spirit: many chapters, for example, make all decisions by consensus. Unlike their anarchist counterparts off-campus, however, student anticorporatists have leaders and spokespeople – and most of them agree that if the movement is to maintain momentum, they will need many more. Fortunately, each major action seems to draw more people in, and new leaders emerge fast – some students who were on the periphery of the Penn group at the February 2000 sit-in, for example, had already assumed official leadership positions within the organization by April of that same year. In part, that was a feature of USAS's anarchic and flexible character – which it shares with the rest of this lively, sometimes militant, radically decentralized global anticorporate movement – a distinct advantage in the high-turnover world of student activism. USAS's commitment to participatory democracy was sorely tested, however, at the group's fractious summer 2000 conference, which was held jointly with 180/Movement for Democracy and Education (MDE) on the University of Oregon's Eugene campus.

The students had very quickly achieved a startling measure of power. Addressing the conference plenary, Thomas Wheatley, a former University of Wisconsin USAS activist who now works for Jobs with Justice in New York City, reflected on the movement's past year: "I didn't think we'd ever get this far. We're really pushing the labor movement forward, and we beat the living shit out of Nike and all kinds of companies."

At the meeting, the big question was, how would students use this new power? How could they work effectively with workers in the global South, make the best use of the newly founded WRC, coordinate campus organizing efforts, and advance their work in coalition with labor unions and others fighting poverty and exploitation in the United States? USAS was growing too, and many members noted at the meeting that it was becoming increasingly complicated to make all decisions through laborious processes of participatory democracy. Conference calls (which cost the organization $25,000 over the 1999–2000 school year), for example, were arranged in the spirit of participatory democracy – any USAS activist can participate, not just a leader or committee member. But many students argued in Eugene that they were not democratic, since they were limited to those who happen to find out about them, or could afford to get on the phone. And some decisions about the national organization, students complained, simply weren't getting made at all. For example, CUNY USAS activist David

Thurston pointed out that USAS was unable to spend money organizing a major presence at national protests in Philadelphia and Los Angeles that summer because no one had the authority to approve such a large financial commitment.

Furthermore, students said, developing relationships with workers in the global South is especially hard without tight structure and nimble coordination. During the spring and summer of 2000, students traveled to Mexico, Nicaragua, and Honduras to meet with labor activists and garment industry workers in those countries and to develop the networks for the nascent Worker Rights Consortium. In March, students investigated a Nike supplier in the Dominican Republic – which made University of Michigan hats – where workers were being fired for attempting to organize unions. USAS activists also met with Dominican workers who were attempting to attend school at night and were consistently prevented from doing so by the factory's practice of forced overtime – production quotas were often impossible to meet within the nine-hour workday. These were promising connections, but the national USAS organization, lacking an infrastructure, had thus far been unable to launch effective campaigns based on what students were learning on these delegations. (This has changed: in 2001, students launched a highly effective campus campaign based on their personal contacts with workers in a Mexican factory; see Chapter 8.) Figuring out a way to do so was an urgent priority at the Eugene meeting.

It was clear to many of the students that they needed to create an organization with some semblance of structure that could, when necessary, allow far-flung and disparate member groups to speak with one voice. But the conference was wracked by bitter conflict over what that structure should look like, and that bitterness reflected acute growing pains in the organization. In particular, passions raged over a proposal to establish an elected governing body that would decide many of the questions that were then being decided on the conference calls, or by (unelected) paid staff in the group's Washington DC office. The anarchists and radical democrats in attendance worried that such a body would turn USAS into a "hierarchical" and "bureaucratic" organization; one even warned, in an address to the plenary, that if the group adopted this structure "we'd be no better than a corporation." Some echoed his anxieties, while others mocked them. George Washington University activist Todd Tucker observed later, "It just seems so stupidly American, like, 'I won't take orders from anyone.' It's John Wayne, not even Bakunin!"

Many advocates of a centralized structure were quick to point out that the students who were most dedicated to USAS tended to support their plan, and that many of those opposing it were fairly peripheral to the organization. Many privately said they were angry that relative outsiders, many of whom weren't familiar with the organization's evolving structure, could have so much influence on a meeting that a hardcore band of committed activists had worked hard to convene.

But other students had a more conflicted view of the anarchists, and of the emerging divisions within the student movement. Anarchists and their ilk have clearly given student organizing an energy and visibility that it hasn't enjoyed in decades. They are, after all, responsible for much of the puppeteering fabulousness that has made "Seattle" and its lesser sequels such media sensations. If the movement alienates the anarchists, worried Marcos de Jesus, a University of Wisconsin–Milwaukee activist, "we won't be the hip new left anymore, we'll just be the boring old left." Many felt that the anarchists brought a radical anticapitalism to the student movement that kept it from becoming too compromised, pre-professional, or dominated by East Coast students, whom many Midwestern and West Coast students see as "elitist." The anarchist influence, many recognize, also helps the movement maintain its independence from unions and other NGOs. Ty Moore, a USAS activist from Oberlin College, is a socialist, not an anarchist, but says he sympathized with their concerns about the "political homogeneity of the national organization."

The controversy over the governing body inspired twenty-nine hours of plenary meetings, two of which lasted past 3 a.m. At several junctures, anarchists walked out of the room and even burst into tears. Taking a cigarette break at the conference, Molly McGrath, who had recently graduated from the University of Wisconsin, and had spent the summer organizing the Eugene conference, sighed with frustration. "It reminds me of the major split in SDS [Students for a Democratic Society]," she said. Indeed, the conflict was in many ways analogous. Like the SDS founders, the anarchists are fiercely dedicated to non-hierarchical structures, but many of their fellow activists − whether liberal or far left − feel that such purism about process and structure conflicts with other movement goals.

Despite the sometimes agonizing conflicts, the students made progress in Eugene. They strategized about how best to finance delegations to overseas sweatshops and about how to build alliances with workers' rights groups. They debated − and passed − a proposal to establish an International Solidarity Committee that would plan the delegations and make sure they were linked to specific campus campaigns. An elected governing body was established, and on the last night those bleary-eyed USAS members who could stand to show up for the last few hours of late-night plenary decided to hold elections later that fall.

A little more than a year later, some semblance of a national structure has been in place since Eugene. Members' skepticism about such hierarchies has eased, but the group is unlikely to become homogenized or bureaucratic. Says national coordinating committee member Dale Weaver, a graduate student at San Jose State who serves on USAS's national coordinating committee, "if there's one thing USAS chapters are, it's independent." Besides, the current leadership seems to have a healthy ambivalence toward its role. Says Santa Clara University's Liana Molina, another coordinating committee member, "The United States is supposedly a democracy and I don't think it's very democratic. So how can we be sure we are representing the members of USAS? We do our best, but it's hard."

Tensions over process do continue to divide the wider student movement. In fall 2001, student anti-war activist conferences in Boston, Berkeley, and elsewhere were completely paralyzed over these questions, as anarchists and radical democrats argued passionately for consensus decision-making while members of the International Socialist Organization, among others, adamantly supported majority voting. From the outside, these can look like trivial sectarian squabbles. But Lara Jiramanus, a recent graduate who is active in Harvard's living-wage campaign and in the Boston Campus Anti-War Coalition, says these debates are far from symbolic: "What is a leader? How should we be treating each other? If we don't ask those questions, we create organizations that no one wants to be part of."

Warning: democracy in process

> Freedom and democracy
> That's the word from
>   Washington everyday
> Puts America to sleep with
>   warm milk and a cliché
> Some people are expendable
>   along the way
> Your dollar is dependable
> What more can we say
>   Ani Di Franco,
>   "Dog Coffee"

"This is what democracy looks like!" people have chanted from Seattle to Genoa, and elsewhere, protesting the World Trade Organization, the International Monetary Fund, and the many other anti-democratic institutions that run the world. Implied in that chant is the notion that we, the demonstrators, have a vision of democracy that differs wildly from that of our world leaders, and, indeed, that democracy is enacted in our activism. It's a powerful idea – but is it true?

When we declare "we" represent "what democracy looks like," we express a powerful desire – one that's not yet a reality. While most USAS activists believe democracy is crucial, it is still a rather amorphous concept for us. With a better understanding of what democracy is in theory and action, we are also better able to imagine a new politics – and we urgently need such vision if our movement is to be sustained.

Democracy in theory

United Students Against Sweatshops, or "the student anti-sweatshop movement," is only a small part of a global movement united, at least in part, by the idea that our democracies are failing to meet their own standards of fairness. A system that perpetuates injustice with an illegitimate use of power is not a fair one – a just system must actively work to end inequalities, or be reinvented. Democracy is more than free elections and fair competition. Francis Moore Lappé once wrote that a true democracy requires that power be accountable to those who live with the consequences of public decisions. The people who work under sweatshop conditions are exploited by unrestrained, unaccountable raw power. Collectively we all struggle, knowing that we must change these pseudo-democratic systems that underlie our massive, global problems.

There are many competing definitions of democracy. Clearly the most mainstream version is a constitutional system of government, divided into executive, legislative, and judicial branches, that check and balance each other by means of being countervailing forces of power. However, a real democracy would depend on a culture of participation beyond what we're taught in the typical classroom. To return to Lappé, a real democracy brings the principles of accountability and shared power into both economic and political life, so citizen participation can flourish – "the essence of freedom". Freedom is not ensured through a vote or protest alone; rather, it is protected by engaged communities. That's what we believe, but can we live it?

Democracy in action

Is your organization plagued by nagging chatter about an "insider/outsider" dynamic? Do your fellow activists think an illegitimate few with overwhelming power run the organization behind the scenes? Do you feel incapable of doing the work someone else has done? How many times have you heard this anxious lament: "What will we do when so-and-so graduates?" Having strong and effective people in our groups is good, but the anxiety of an organizational meltdown when they leave haunts us. Democracy's broad, underlying principles need to inform our work. And when they don't, our organizations suffer the consequences.

Sociologists have known for a long time that organizations have difficulties with internal democracy. Instinctively, they prioritize the preservation of "leader power" and "organizational survival," sometimes even if that means sacrificing the original organizational mission. We are generally very uncomfortable with such dynamics, yet too often we permit them because, living in an undemocratic society, we haven't been prepared to function democratically. Democratic process is not given to us: we have to create it and it's difficult.

The plethora of people that make up the "student anti-sweatshop movement" were made keenly aware of organizational issues surrounding democracy at our Summer Conference 2000 in Eugene, Oregon. There we debated and debated, into the early hours of the morning, the significance of the positions of responsibility in an organization. As we grappled with the implications of creating positions that imply power, hierarchy, and perhaps domination, we worried and disagreed about the consequence. There is a tendency in our society to define an organization as something hierarchically directed, with a clear-cut, central leadership. Many think the only alternative to this is no organization at all. This is a false dichotomy. In USAS, we've seen that our organization is at its best when individuals assume – often temporary – positions of coordination and responsibility. Our term for such a

Tulane students during their sit-in in March 2000, debating strategy

position is "bottom-liner." It is a compromise between anarchy and leader-domination.

I've seen USAS take many different forms. We've been a mass of people affiliated only by conference calls that stretched on for hours. We've been U-locked, back-to-back, in the chancellor's office, during an occupation to secure our university's membership in the Worker's Rights Consortium. We've been in Washington DC, at the protests of the International Monetary Fund and the World Bank, desperately trying to find some meaning in the sudden plethora of massive, international protests. And we've been a series of rather unorganized committees, which is probably where most of the work in USAS is actually accomplished. All of these forms of organization are legitimate, but only if we maintain a strong commitment to internal democracy. And that means we must make an effort to share power within our organization.

Organizational democracy means understanding that anyone can learn what you've learned. You may think you should monopolize the challenging leadership role, because you know you can do it, but from the standpoint of democracy you should not. We must share knowledge and skills — especially in an organization where the learning curve is short and fast, and where the questions that we ask, and the challenges that we accept, are not easy ones. We must remember that values do not need to be sacrificed for the social imperative. Move slowly. Take a step back and imagine a yellow sign that says, "Warning: Democracy in Process." In a movement where our numbers are so crucially lacking, we can't afford not to do everything we can to bring new people in.

Unfettered economic power undermines democracy, creating a climate ripe for exploitation. Corporate conglomerates like Nike rake in billions in profit each year while the people who sew our clothes may earn less than a dollar a day, and are denied the right to form independent unions. And in our zeal to right these global wrongs, our commitment to principles of democracy in our work can waver. Think coordination. Think responsibility. And think education.

The anticorporate globalization movement is entering a new phase in this time of war, so we must keep our minds open to new political possibilities. Democracy is not just a buzzword in a chant. Its meaning extends from political and economic equality to committing yourself to sharing your knowledge and skills with as many people as you can. Now more than ever, we need to put theory into action: in our so-called democratic societies, and in our own organizations.

Molly McGrath

six

"Not so cute any more": USAS and the politics of race

Unlike that of the 1960s, today's student movement is unlikely to be destroyed by disagreements over ideology and structure. But, like the movements of the 1960s, it is marred by formidable racial tensions. While USAS, and the rest of the predominately white anticorporate movement have done admirable work on solidarity across national borders and the divides of social class, race has proven a more difficult chasm to cross, especially among fellow student activists. Students of color are organizing; in recent years, they have been protesting the repeal of affirmative action in Florida's and California's state universities, the dearth of campus services for minority students, and inadequate African-American Studies curricula. In New York State and California, they have protested the state's funding priorities: spending on prisons at the expense of higher education.

Some of this organizing has been strikingly successful. In late spring 2001 at Penn State, the administration repeatedly failed to respond to racist death threats against black students, including the president of the Black Caucus. (Those threats included a reference to a dead black man's body in the woods, *a body which was later found*.) Five thousand Penn State students of all races showed up to a rally protesting the administration's failure to act, and in support of the Black Caucus's demands, which included an Africana Studies Research Center and other academic improvements. For nine days, 300–500 students per night camped out in the student union – many on hunger strike – and the occupation ended in victory. The administration ended up meeting most of the Black Caucus's demands, and the event suggested the tremendous potential of an emerging campus civil rights movement.

Yet the relationship of anti-racist activists to anticorporate groups like USAS can be uneasy. Indeed, as Daraka Larimore-Hall and Tracie McMillan point out in the Summer 2001 issue of *The Activist*, the official publication of Young Democratic Socialists of America, there are two distinct student movements, with sadly few coalitions bridging the divide.

Students of color recognize connections between racism and global economic exploitation. Farah Mongeau, a University of Michigan law student and member of UM's Students of Color Coalition (SCC), points out, "Sweatshop labor obviously affects people of color. People of color are the ones who work in the sweatshops." Yet "people of color" is a broad, often unhelpful category, and, as the racial makeup of most campus anti-sweatshop groups suggests, it doesn't necessarily lend itself to easy transnational solidarity.

Some students of color locate the estrangement in inequality: white activists receive better treatment from those in power. At Michigan in February 2000, SCC members protesting a racist secret society held a sit-in at the same time as the anti-sweat organization and resented the fact that while they were ignored for weeks, the predominantly white group got a meeting with the president immediately. Students of color involved in other anticorporate globalization activism also express concern that they will be received differently – perhaps to lethal effect. Justin Higgins was sophomore class president at North Carolina Central University, a historically black college, when interviewed in winter 2000. He had just joined the regional student anti-WTO/IMF coalition, but said he wasn't planning to go to Washington DC that spring, and wasn't sorry to have missed Seattle. "If there had been black students [in Seattle]," Higgins said, "there would have been real bullets, not rubber bullets." Similarly, Tshaka Barrows, president of the Black Students Association, visited the protesters at UW Madison's first anti-sweatshop sit-in with his BSA colleagues. "We are with you in your fight against exploitation," he said, but added that they wouldn't be sticking around, because they were afraid the cops would show up.

White students are also likely to receive more media coverage – and that, too, breeds resentment. Despite its large scale and its success, Penn State events got little national press coverage, especially when compared to a Harvard occupation going on at exactly the same time.

There are also social divisions. Bhumika Muchhala, a recent graduate who is now working full-time in USAS's national office, says anti-sweatshop activism can be "cliquish." She describes a close-knit, white hippie activist culture that is "not welcoming to people of color." As a student activist, she says, "I had two sets of friends, my Indian friends and my activist friends." Dave Thurston, a black USAS activist who attends CUNY's Hunter College, agrees that the organization can be inhospitably white and middle-class, semi-indignantly citing the all-vegan food at conferences. "Oh my fucking word," he sighs, "and twinkling!" (Twinkling is a hand gesture that comes from the Quakers, used to signify assent without disrupting the meeting or repeating what they've said; while many find it useful, it can feel alienating to outsiders, and is often cited as a symbol of the odd, cultish behavior of white activists.)

The divide also, in USAS's case, has to do with the group's origins in privilege. Anti-sweatshop activism, like most concern about faraway poor people, comes out of a sense of one's own advantage and comfort, and many black students don't feel comfortable on today's campus, even if they are middle class. The death threats at Penn State offer some clue as to why that might be. Students of color often feel that they are, as one black UNC graduate put it, "constantly under siege." Like working-class students working full-time to cover skyrocketing tuition fees, they don't have the luxury of organizing on behalf of others. (Of course, many students of color are also working class.) In part, that has to do with the limits of anticorporatism, as discussed in Chapter 3; it focuses on an external enemy, while fighting racism involves changing ourselves. Racism is rooted in large power structures, of course, but it is also about everyday interactions and relationships. While anticorporatism tends to absolve the privileged from responsibility – unless they own a corporation – antiracist struggles do hold white people responsible.

Some student activists of color sense that white student activists work on Third World issues because domestic issues in the US, almost by definition, involve race, which white people don't want to talk about. Feeling that student activists have empathized with the sufferings of workers in Indonesia and Thailand while overlooking those of their African-American neighbors and fellow citizens, some have even implied racism in white student activists' focus on overseas sweatshops. During a panel at USAS's 2000 national conference, David Thurston pointed out that "people don't have the same kind of sympathy for prisoners as sweatshop workers." Hanna Jones, a University of Massachusetts–Amherst student starting an anti-prison group on her campus, agreed, and thought it was because so many prisoners are black. "I'm probably going to piss a lot of people off," said Jones, who is African American, "but I think that's a race issue. We're talking about racism that has not been resolved."

To many students of color, anti-sweatshop activism seems a dodge from injustice at home. African-American UNC–Chapel Hill activist Erica Smiley, who had been a leader in a campaign against a tuition hike, and whose winter 2000 campaign for student body president galvanized a progressive multiracial coalition that is unusual on the US campus, was annoyed by USAS. They get so much recognition, she said, for being "cute white kids protesting injustices that are *far away*." Interviewed during her campaign, Smiley said she wished USAS activists would direct their energies toward US social problems. "When they do that," she laughed, "shit's going to go *down*. They're not going to be so cute any more."

Since that interview, Smiley's wish has gradually come true. Many USAS activists are leading living-wage campaigns, in close solidarity with workers on their campuses. USAS activists in California have extensive alliances with student and youth prison activists. This reflects an increased interest in injustice at home in the student anticorporate movement, an impulse that may translate into better coalition-building. New multiracial corporate campaigns are emerging, like the Taco Bell boycott, which highlights the chain's mistreatment of migrant farm workers. At the Democratic and Republican national convention protests of 2000, as well as the 2001 inauguration protests, matters of racial justice – the death penalty, prison population growth, police brutality, voting rights – shared the stage with abuses of corporate power. These protests drew a far more racially and economically diverse crowd of students and youth than others, like Seattle and A16, which had focused almost exclusively on abuse of corporate power overseas. And while USAS membership remains whiter than most people – inside and outside the organization – think it should be, the national leadership in fall 2001 boasted many more students of color than it had the year before. That could have a significant effect on USAS's organizational culture.

Still, for the most part, neither USAS, nor the rest of the anticorporate movement have figured out how to form lasting coalitions with student civil rights organization, led by student activists of color. But if they do, some shit really will go down.

Testimony from students at the Penn State sleep-out

"I was only planning to attend the rally on Tuesday for 15 minutes, but after I started hearing the stories people had to tell, I stayed her for 30 hours.... I've only left to get a sleeping bag. I missed a quiz, but other than sleep, I'm not missing anything, and missing sleep is not a big deal at all for a cause like this."

Griffin Oesterle

"I'm scared for my life and feel that if we all stay together we can accomplish something. IT'S NOT OVER! We want answers. I've slept four hours in the past four days for this cause, and I'm proud of it!"

Carlyne Sainphor

"Why would someone not come? It stresses diversity and the ability to rise above hatred. *It's the best thing I've ever done at Penn State.* Numbers count, one person counts. I haven't slept in 45 hours, missed a staff meeting and some classes, but the Black Caucus has worked all year; certainly we can spare a few days to show student support."

Leah Bragin

"This [rally] is the best education I've had in four years of school. For the first time, I'm proud to be a Penn State student."

Jordan Dershaw

seven

"Where's your activism?" USAS and feminism

In the recent history of student activism, the new emphasis on economics, which emerged in the late 1990s, represented quite a shift. At the beginning of that decade, there was plenty of student organizing, but it was fragmentary and sporadic, and most of it focused on what some, mostly its detractors, liked to call "identity politics," fighting the oppression of racial and sexual minorities, and of women. Admirable as they were – and effective in improving social relations on many campuses – there was little sense of solidarity among these groups, and they often seemed insular, bearing little relation to life outside the university.

That political moment ended in the mid 1990s, partly because in the larger world organized feminism was in a lull and the mainstream gay movement was focusing on issues like inclusion in the military, gay marriage, and hate-crimes legislation – moderate goals that don't speak to student idealism. It's also because from 1993 to 2001, with a Democrat in the White House, and the religious right in retreat, gay life – like abortion rights – seemed less precarious. By contrast, among the young, the economic left – especially the labor movement, and the burgeoning resistance to global capital – enjoyed a resurgence, both in numbers and in vision.

But the struggles of the early 1990s over gender and sexuality haven't vanished without a trace; indeed, it sometimes seems as if, through the anticorporate movement, they have returned to their roots as movements for radical liberation. There are few active campus groups focusing on the struggle against homophobia. But the tactics – militant, theatrical, and often campy direct action – of early-1990s groups like ACT UP and Queer Nation have clearly influenced the new crew of student activists. The most memorable demonstrators at the 2000 Republican convention in Philadelphia, for example, were the Billionaires for Bush (or Gore), who wore tuxes and pearls and chanted: "What do we want? Prison labor! How do we want it? Cheap!" In a similarly saucy vein, anti-fashion shows have become a common staple of the anti-sweatshop protests. USAS, many of whose members are gay, lesbian or bisexual, has active Queer and Women's Caucuses and takes an aggressive approach to combating homophobia and sexism within the organization. Kitty Krupat, a labor activist and editor of the anthology *Out at Work: Building a Gay-Labor Alliance*, sees in USAS's "persistent interest" in these issues an attempt to integrate labor and identity-based movements.

It is abundantly clear that the visibility of campus groups devoted solely to "women's" issues – like abortion rights and sexual assault – waned during the Clinton years, leading many, both in the media and in the women's movement, to fear that feminist organizing was on the decline among students. In 1998, *Time* magazine asked "Is Feminism Dead?" Left feminist writer Katha Pollitt, writing in 1999, echoed this, asking the younger generation of feminists "Where's your activism?"

These commentators were on to something. Under Clinton, rightly or wrongly, many college-aged women grew complacent about abortion rights; this hurt campus feminism, as it hurt many mainstream feminist organizations which had, in the Reagan–Bush years, devoted most of their resources and passion to the issue.

But rumors of campus feminism's death were much exaggerated. Many college-aged women, far from taking feminist gains for granted, are joining the global women's movement against poverty. That movement includes anti-poverty activists fighting so-called "welfare reform," and female workers, both in the US and in the global South, who are organizing to improve their own work conditions. The movement against corporate globalization, too, has an increasingly explicit feminist component; many women, for example, organized feminist affinity groups for April 2001's Quebec City protest against the FTAA, to make clear that the burden of global poverty falls disproportionately on women.

USAS is part of this phenomenon, frequently emphasizing that 90 percent of garment factory workers are women. Pushing for women's rights clauses in codes of conduct, students frequently point to the gender discrimination these workers face: UNITE has reported wage discrimination in the Dominican Republic and elsewhere, while NLC has reported that forced pregnancy tests and injection of workers with contraceptives are common in the maquiladoras. And workers have sometimes been influenced by their USAS allies to make their own feminist ideals more explicit. A group of workers organizing an independent union in a Mexican factory, inspired by a discussion with a USAS delegation, added provisions to their new union's bylaws forbidding sexual harassment among members, and stipulating that half the union's elected positions be held by women.

Of course, despite its feminist analysis and mission, USAS does not always function in a way that makes its feminist members happy. Among the organization's leadership, women feel that men leave much of the undesirable work up to them, and men are often more recognized – both publicly (they tend to be quoted more in media reports) and within the organization.

One of the most interesting aspects of USAS's feminism has been its approach to the representation of sweatshop workers. Some Western labor advocates and anti-globalization scholars, including the otherwise admirable National Labor Committee, have tended to portray the women who work in sweatshops as helpless victims, dependent on Western activists to save them. The Western anti-sweatshop movement has "a lot of problems with patriarchal and colonial attitudes towards garment workers," says Molly McGrath. "Groups such as the NLC rarely portray garment workers in a way other than 'thousands of desperate workers with no control over their lives who are starving to death'. This rhetoric has a huge impact on the anti-sweatshop campaigns in the US – with religious groups, unions, and human rights-advocacy groups." Such language helps hook people in, students say, but is not the stuff of which solidarity is made.

Bangladeshi scholar Naila Kabeer's 2000 book *The Power to Choose: Bangladeshi Women and Labor Market Decisions in London and Dhaka* helps explain why this is. "In comparison to the detailed attention paid to employers' motivations in hiring a young and female work force," she writes, criticizing scholars' representations of female Third World workers, "there was a deafening silence on who these women were, why they had sought factory employment and what their jobs meant to them ... such approaches attributed far more animation and personality to capital than to the female labour it exploited." Kabeer extends that criticism to First World labor advocates – she focuses on those working on Britain's Clean Clothes campaign, but unfortunately, it applies to many other efforts – who have often used dehumanizing terms like "cheap labor" to describe Third World workers. Such representation ignores these women's own struggles for self-determination, and reinforces degrading stereotypes about the passivity of Third World, especially Asian, women.

Such images can easily be used against the women, even as they are intended to evoke sympathy. As Kabeer points out, images of passive Asians have often been used by First World labor groups in protectionist campaigns, whose message is that hiring Third World women is inherently objectionable, because, the implication is, these workers could only be exploited. Such representations seem to foreclose the possibility that such workers could work, and bargain over their labor, with dignity.

USAS activists, often informed by classroom exposure to Women's Studies, agree with such critiques of First World anti-sweatshop language, and, along with feminist organizations like STITCH, have brought a feminist, anti-colonialist analysis to a North American movement that was sorely lacking one. Says McGrath, "We have put more analysis into the way we are representing these relationships, and have tried to change the rhetoric to show sweatshop workers with more agency and power."

To some USAS activists, this emphasis comes not only from thinking and reading about these ideas, but also from their own experience. For some working-class students, especially Latinas or Asian women, the issue of objectifying workers is hardly academic. "We have a more visceral reaction," says Evelyn Zepeda of Pitzer College. A garment worker, she says, "could be my mom."

For others, this perspective has evolved out of their anti-sweatshop activism, and out of visits to workers. On a recent USAS delegation to Mexico, students and workers played riotous midnight soccer games and stayed up late dancing together and hanging out; students learned, too, that despite their difficult circumstances, not all sweatshop workers' lives were miserable. "They treat that factory like a high school," says Zepeda of the teenage workers, who spend as much of the day as they can flirting and gossiping.

The "change" in representation to which McGrath refers is apparent in USAS activists' public reports on delegation visits to other countries. For instance, on the University of Arizona's Students Against Sweatshops website, SAS member Rachel Wilson posted photos from her trip to Kukdong, a factory in Puebla, Mexico, that makes sweatshirts for the University of Arizona and other colleges. In contrast with the NLC's website, not a single photo shows a worker looking beaten down or demoralized. The sixteen- and seventeen-year-old workers wear sweatshirts and look very much like American teenagers; in some pictures, it is hard to tell them from the college students in USAS's multiracial delegation. Throughout, Wilson's photos and text emphasize the workers' effort to start an independent union, who they are as individuals, and what their work and their activism means to them. These profiles give us a vivid sense of the real people involved in this struggle. Josefina Hernandez, for example, a big, maternal-looking union activist who at twenty-eight "is considered the 'old lady' of the group," is wearing a T-shirt that says "Shut Up and Drive." Wilson's caption tells us that when police raided the factory during a strike earlier this year, "Josefina protected many young girls." A caption of a photo showing Wilson and Hernandez laughing and chatting over breakfast tells us more about Josefina:

> She says that despite everything, she loves Kukdong. That is where she learned to sew and become independent. She says she was always a troublemaker in school, but now she's found an appropriate outlet for her spirit: union organizing.

Represented this way, with the emphasis on their humanity and their power rather than on their suffering, sweatshop workers seem more real, even to a privileged First World audience. In fact, their problems seem much like those that befall the average American – bad workplace conditions and the repression of trade-union rights. Such identification bodes far better for global solidarity than what early UNC–Chapel Hill USAS activist Marion Traub-Werner calls the rhetoric of "victimization." In the absence of such solidarity, Molly McGrath points out that the sad stories of the sweatshop don't mean much to the public; its abuses become "yet another horrible global problem to ignore."

Better representation of workers can also provide a helpful corrective to the larger anti-globalization movement, which, ignoring the perspective of women workers, at times assumes that "globalization" is an unwelcome intrusion into Third World countries. Yet for women in the developing world, factory jobs can offer a way out of patriarchal family or village roles. Women in Bangladesh, for example, often face extreme disapproval from husbands and fathers for accepting work in factories, even when their families need the money. Men (accurately) view women's factory work as a move outside the domestic sphere and a threat to their own authority in every sense; thus, rumors of sexual promiscuity among female garment workers are rampant in Bangladesh, as they are on the Mexican border and elsewhere. But like Josefina Hernandez in Mexico, Bangladeshi women often equate garment industry work with independence, and that's one reason so many choose it.

An understanding of these issues has led USAS to focus on issues that differ from those that interest more mainstream anti-sweatshop groups. The organization's approach to young workers, for instance, resists paternalism. Evelyn Zepeda cringes, describing one North American union's "help" on the USAS campaign to support striking workers at Kukdong. Picking up on a report that young teenagers worked in the plant, the union sent out an alarmist press release accusing the company of tolerating "child labor." But USAS does not base campaigns on the child labor issue, both because its sensationalism tends to obscure more important matters like freedom of association, and because the organization recognizes that there are no easy answers. Girls in developing countries frequently lie about their age to obtain factory employment; what business do Western labor advocates have, many student activists reason, "protecting" them if they want to work? Zepeda says, "We understand that families may need the money." After that incident, USAS kept that union from playing any significant strategic role in the campaign. Zepeda laughs, "We let them buy us a computer."

As Michael Hardt and Antonio Negri point out in *Empire*, those waging war on global capital shouldn't defend the oppressive systems it has been steadily displacing; indeed, they should regard those past world orders – whether feudalism, theocracy, or patriarchy – with a "healthy and lucid disgust." In that spirit, USAS has been standing side by side with women who are defending their rights to earn their living in the global economy *and* to force that economy to treat them with the respect they deserve.

Yesenia's story

Yesenia Bonilla is from Lima, Honduras. Yesenia started working in a maquila factory called KIMI when she was sixteen and soon became a leader of the nascent union in the factory. This testimony was taken one month after Hurricane Mitch devastated the region, in December 1998. The union finally won a collective bargaining agreement in March 1999, securing some of the best living conditions in the region for themselves and their families. In May of 2000, KIMI de Honduras closed its doors and moved its production to Modas Cielo, a non-union factory in Guatemala. Research revealed that KIMI produces collegiate apparel. At the time of writing, USAS students are using the Code of Conduct to pressure KIMI and its business partners to respect the right to organize in their supplier's factory. When she was twenty-four, Yesenia told her story to Marion Traub-Werner, a founding member of USAS who was at that time working for Support Team International for Textileras (STITCH), a women's labor solidarity organization.

I started working at KIMI when I was sixteen. I live with six brothers and sisters, as well as my father and mother, and my sister's daughter. When you're the oldest in a large family there's not much choice but to work to support the family. So I left school to help out. Besides my father, three of us kids work. We have been able to send two of our sisters to school for two years this way.

It wasn't easy to get the job at KIMI. The woman in charge of hiring said, "No, little one, you are too young," and escorted me right out of the industrial park. She said the boss didn't want to hire minors because he didn't want to give them all the legal benefits. He wanted them to work the same hours as everyone else.

It was three months before I managed to get them to hire me. I got to know one of the guards at the park, and he snuck me in one day. I went back to KIMI because that's where my mother was working. By that time there was a new director of personnel. He took one look at me and said, "You're very young, but I'll see what I can do." He gave me some tests and when he saw that I could do the work, he gave me my needle. That's how I got into the maquila at sixteen.

I was happy to get the job, but it was also bad luck in a way because of the abuse we've had to endure at KIMI. My first job was cutting cloth. I only did that for two days. On the third day, a Korean supervisor, who was very tough, put me on a machine attaching sleeves. She wanted to take advantage of me because I was so young. She insulted me, made me cry, and hit me. She threw pieces of cloth in my face and demanded that I attach sleeves as fast as the more experienced workers. My mother worked in KIMI at this time. She saw how the Korean supervisor mistreated me just because I was the newest and youngest in the line. She challenged her, right there in front of everyone. For that, they fired my mother. And when she went to look for work at other maquilas, they wouldn't hire her. They said she was too old. They don't let a person of forty or forty-five work in the maquila.

We endured a lot of abuse. We started work at 7 in the morning and wouldn't finish until late at night. There was no scheduled time when our shift ended. That made it very difficult for the people who lived far away. Another problem was that the company didn't provide purified water. The water was really dirty. But the worst problem was how they treated us. Like I told you, supervisors would hit us with the fabric pieces. They'd throw them in our faces and swear at us.

So in 1994, we decided to organize a union. I was seventeen when I joined and had only been working with the company for five months. I didn't really know what a union was, so I asked my father. He told me that a union was a good thing, and that I should go and see what I could do.

The executive committee held meetings in a room three or four blocks away from my house, so I went. They talked with us about what the union could do to help the workers. They also taught us about the labor laws. At first, I was afraid. But later I thought, why should I be afraid? Legal is legal, and I'm really only defending the laws of our country. Once I understood what unions could mean for workers, I was able to recruit a lot of *compañeras*. We organized almost the whole industrial park, but unfortunately in Honduras the laws favor the bosses and not the workers. The company fired our first executive committee and that really weakened our union.

But we did make some gains. We got purified water; the company started to pay for transportation; and they also fixed the road to the factory, which used to be horrible. They put in lights so it wasn't so dark for the workers who had to walk home late at night. But it didn't take long before they forgot all that and started treating us badly again. They took away our transportation and the other things we had gained.

In 1996, we started to organize again. We organized a work stop-

Ngadinah Mawardi, an Indonesian garment worker and union organizer

page involving workers from all the factories in the park. In response, KIMI management fired the executive committee and sixteen other workers, including myself. We had been out of work for a month and a half, when the company decided to fire forty-eight more workers who had continued to organize inside the plant.

That's when we called a strike. It started on October 7 and finished October 12. Through the strike we won recognition of our union. Without the strike, we couldn't have done it. The company was also forced to reinstate all of us with full back pay. After we got our legal status, I became one of the first members of the executive committee. I was re-elected twice, and, thanks to God, we have won a lot of things for the workers.

You know, I was so shy when I started. Almost everything that the boss did to me made me cry. But I learned that you have to defend your rights, not with obscene words but in a dignified way. To me a trade unionist is a person who is very responsible, who has to leave her fear behind and speak frankly with the boss. What we ask is that the bosses respect the rights of the other workers.

At KIMI, the managers try to scare you. The Korean supervisors especially insult union members on the factory floor in front of everyone. And what does the director of personnel do? He just laughs. It's all to discredit the union. The result is that the workers start to think the union isn't good for anything, that it's more trouble than it's worth.

They harass us in other ways as well. For several years, I was able to work overtime, but that stopped as soon as I became a member of the union executive committee. For the past two years, management has denied union leadership overtime.

Being a trade unionist is seen as a betrayal by the boss. Why? Because as trade unionists we insist that the company apply the laws, and we struggle for all the workers whether they are union members or not. That's not good for the bosses.

The union has taken up many struggles this year. We have fought to get the company to give young workers permission to leave at 4:30 instead of 5:30 p.m., so they would have enough time to get to night school. And we are still fighting for our contract. We want to improve many things, especially the salary. Our base rate is about 350 lempiras [US$25.35] a week. We get a daily attendance bonus and a weekly production bonus for meeting the production quotas. If the garment style is simple, it's easy to make the quota, and you can earn as much as 400 or 420 lempiras [US$29 or US$30] for a six-day week.

But if you miss a day, they take away all your bonuses and deduct two days of pay. And we don't have any sick leave. For missing one day, even if you are sick, you lose about half your salary for that week. It's not unusual to earn as little as 200 lempiras [US$14.50]. That is very hard for us. Many of the workers are single mothers and sometimes they need to take their children to the doctor.

So, we were supposed to negotiate the last few clauses of the contract the day the hurricane hit. Now, the company is taking advantage of the situation to stop negotiations and has temporarily suspended many of the workers. Especially now, in these times, workers need their salaries. Many were left without homes.

Another issue in the maquila is health. During the seven years I have worked at KIMI, I have been sick with bronchitis a number of times. My lungs have been very affected by the dust, and by all the pressure from the bosses. If you don't make the production quota, they punish you. So in order to meet the quota, you have to run out and eat real quick at midday and return right away to get back to work. All that pressure gives you gastritis, which I've had quite a few times.

The fact is that the quota is too high, although management keeps saying it is too low. But as we have said to the bosses, it's the woman sitting at the machine who knows whether the quota is realistic or not, who knows whether it's humanly possible to meet the quota or not. A boss may know how to calculate how much time it takes, but it's the

workers who know what's possible and what the health problems are. All the bosses know is what quota and quality they want.

That's why we say that, yes, the maquila has brought work, but it has also brought sickness. When you start working in a maquila you're young, healthy and filled with life. But workers leave the maquilas sick.

I'd like to leave the maquila one day. I would like to study and to be able to have a better job. I went to school up to the sixth grade. Now I would like to prepare myself, and perhaps go to university. That would be great. Of course, right now that's not possible. It is really difficult trying to study and work in the maquila at the same time. With a collective agreement, maybe we could do that.

You know, for the past seven years, since I was sixteen, I have worked in a maquila almost seven days a week. Of course it makes you tougher. But after so many years in the same job, you want a better job. But if you don't have the opportunity to study, it's just not possible. Perhaps you don't have any support, like your parents can't help because they have too many children or because their jobs don't pay enough. But, yes, one day I will do it. I will get an education. Maybe I'll even go and work in other countries, who knows?

eight

"Sí, se puede!"
USAS and solidarity

In January 2001, over 850 workers at Kukdong International Mexico, a Korean-owned garment factory in Atlixco de Puebla, went on strike when five of their co-workers were illegally fired for trying to organize an independent union. During an occupation of the factory, in which workers peacefully protested the firings, riot police violently assaulted workers. Since Kukdong contracts with Nike and Reebok to make sweatshirts bearing the logos of the Universities of North Carolina–Chapel Hill, Michigan, Oregon and many other schools boasting active anti-sweatshop groups, the conflict couldn't have presented a better test case for the effectiveness of the student anti-sweatshop movement. The Kukdong struggle, said Eric Brakken in February, is "the most important thing we've been a part of. If we win here, it's the beginning of a real international strategy."

Like many Mexican workers, Kukdong employees were at that time forced to belong to a mafia union with close ties to management and to the local government, which pays supervisors to support it, resists dissent with brutal violence, and had never been supported by a majority of the factory's workers. The Kukdong workers, 90 percent of whom are young women, knew they needed a union of their own, because the mob union – Revolutionary Confederation of Workers and Peasants, or FCROC – had failed to respond to any of their complaints, and they were getting desperate. "From what I see, the FCROC works only for the factory," sixteen-year-old Kukdong worker Juana Hernandez said in an interview with USAS researchers. Alvaro Saaveda Anzures, also sixteen, agreed: "The FCROC is a union in appearance only."

Wages at the factory, most workers say, are insufficient to support a single person, much less someone with children or dependants. Conditions at the factory were abominable as well; many workers accepted the job because management had promised free breakfasts and lunch, but the food Kukdong provided was insufficient and, even worse, rancid and worm-infested. "I was sick for three days from the food I ate there," Alvaro Saavedra told USAS. According to copiously sourced WRC reports – based on extensive interviews with workers and management – the Kukdong employees were also subjected to verbal and physical abuse, even hit with hammers and screwdrivers. The Kukdong factory was in clear violation, the WRC found, of the WRC's code of conduct, and those of its member universities.

The workers' organizing grew out of talks with USAS activists, one of whom, David Alvarado, had been living in Puebla. The Kukdong workers decided to push for an independent union – an extremely bold and risky step in the maquila – because they knew they had powerful allies in USAS and the WRC. When the workers went on strike, students picketed Nike stores in several cities, and on campuses nationwide urged administrators to pressure Nike and Reebok. After widely publicized WRC investigations (whose findings were largely confirmed by Verité, a monitor hired by Nike and Reebok), local media coverage and agitation from students, university administrators and labor activists worldwide, Nike and Reebok intervened. The companies initially, of course, did nothing; however, eventually the sneaker titans forced Kukdong management to rehire a majority of the fired workers, including two of the union leaders, within two months of the dismissals.

Against all odds, the workers and students have won. According to a WRC report released in late June 2001, their combined agitation had resulted in better food, wage increases for some workers, the apparent abolition of physical abuse, and improved sanitary conditions. Even more surprisingly, the FCROC voluntarily left the factory that summer; management recognized that a majority of the workers support SITEKIM, and at the time of writing, workers and management were about to begin negotiating a collective bargaining agreement. At USAS's instigation, US Representative George Miller visited Puebla in early September, and received a commitment from the governor of Puebla to grant SITEKIM official recognition. (Early USAS activist Tico Almeida was working in Miller's office and brought the situation to the congressman's attention.) SITEKIM will be the first independent union in the Mexican maquila, and one of the few democratic unions chosen by the workers themselves. To celebrate the victory, USAS activists and workers from Kukdong (now called Mexmode, due to a factory name-change in fall 2001) went on a speaking tour in late November/early December, visiting a dozen US colleges, and emphasizing the influence universities can have in improving working conditions overseas.

It is clear that Nike's interventions, though never as timely or as aggressive as workers and students would have liked, made all the difference. In spring 2001, in response to students' exhortations not to "cut and run," both Nike and Reebok publicly committed to keeping production in Atlixco de Puebla. Of Nike's involvement, Eric Brakken of USAS said, "It's interesting, I think we've scared the fuck out of them." Like most corporate fears, however, this one needs to be constantly stoked. As this book goes to press, Reebok continues to place orders at the factory. USAS and the WRC are maintaining a constant presence at Kukdong and activists nationwide will continue to pressure university administrators and Nike to ensure that the factory bargains in good faith. Throughout the fall, Nike appeared to be trying hard to extricate itself from this role, and the company placed no orders at the factory. But at the end of November, after months of student pressure, Nike sent a letter to college administrators announcing its intentions to begin contracting with the factory again – in spring 2002. Clearly workers and students will have to be willing to keep constant pressure on Nike, to ensure that the workers don't pay for their victory with their jobs.

In March 2001, while one USAS delegation was visiting Atlixco de Puebla, another traveled to Derby – a town near Buffalo, New York – to investigate allegations of workers'-rights violations in the aptly named New Era factory, which makes hats for several US universities. USAS activists, interviewing nearly thirty workers, as well as several local officials, found that the company was responding to New Era workers' recent unionization with the Communications Workers of America (CWA) by laying off two-thirds of the workforce, shifting production to its non-unionized factories and drastically cutting wages. The company, which had, during the union drive, illegally fired union leaders and threatened others with plant closings, has also failed to provide adequate compensation for its many workers who have been injured on the job. Just as Kukdong management justified its abuses of Mexican workers by citing the hard work and greater "efficiency" of its Indonesian workforce, New Era claimed its unionized employees in western New York weren't competitive with lower-paid workers in Alabama or Bangladesh.

USAS is now calling on universities to use their relationship with New Era to pressure the company to stop the layoffs and wage cuts, rehire workers, and honor their freedom of association. CWA, recognizing the potential of its student allies, has hired a full-time campus organizer to work on the New Era campaign. In fall 2001, workers at New Era went on strike, protesting a 30 percent pay cut and continued safety and health violations; USAS held solidarity actions on campuses nationwide.

These battles represent a profound evolution in the anti-sweatshop movement's approach. Appropriately, while USAS's summer 2000 conference had emphasized the movement's internal dynamics, the theme of the summer 2001 conference was "solidarity," because the organization owes its success to its evolving relationships with workers and other activists. Indeed, the future of the anti-sweatshop movement lies in such relationships. USAS has shown that it is possible for consumers to work effectively, not on behalf of workers, but in solidarity with their struggles.

The New Era and Kukdong struggles underscore another of the group's most promising new tendencies. Like the activists worldwide who fight neighborhood gentrification and water privatization in between World Bank meetings, USAS is learning to connect the global and the local. Corporations certainly do. New Era constantly – and illegally – threatens its employees with globalization: if they make trouble, production will move elsewhere and they'll lose their jobs. Telling his employees to vote against the union, the CFO told them that the company was "going global." Longtime New Era worker Terry Hilburger told USAS investigators, "I had no idea what that meant. I thought, oh, good, we're going to get lots of orders from everywhere, lots of work in the plant. But going global meant getting workers in Bangladesh to make the caps for 89 cents … [New Era is] making millions here, but they want more millions."

USAS, along with a growing economic justice movement, is seeking a better kind of globalization. In an August 14, 2001 story on USAS's triumphs at Kukdong, a dulcet-voiced NPR reporter praised Nike for its role in improving the situation, and said the events showed that "globalization can be a force for positive change." One doesn't have to share her excessive affection for – and trust in – transnational corporations to agree with that sentiment. Like the corporations they're fighting, USAS and its allies are "going global," working towards the internationalization of resistance. In a May Day letter from SITEKIM to USAS, workers wrote:

> We know that at times our faith is lost, but as long as we are together with each other, we will give each other the spirit to move forward, because we know what we do will be good for others in any part of the world.

As tends to happen in politics, the old has become new again. The international solidarity that was so central to past workers' movements and rhetoric makes more sense than ever. In speeches by labor bureaucrats and even liberal politicians like Cynthia McKinney, the phrase "Workers of the world unite!" has been making a decidedly non-ironic comeback. So has another venerable slogan of struggle. Capturing both the optimism and the internationalism of the anti-sweatshop movement, the Mexmode workers ended their May Day letter with their new union's old-time motto, now frequently heard at student, labor and immigrant rights rallies this side of the border: "Sí, se puede!"

These interviews with Kukdong workers were conducted by USAS activists Elizabeth Brennan, Taylor Khym, Bennett Baumer, and David Alvarado, a few months before the workers' independent union won recognition.

Marcela Muñoz, Sewing supervisor, line 14, Chietla

From the beginning Marcela, a SITEKIM leader, has played an integral role in organizing fellow workers at Kukdong. When she is not working at the factory, she travels from town to town organizing workers in their homes. Marcela is a 22-year-old single mother who hardly gets to see her three-year-old son, Luis Eduardo. She lives two hours from Kukdong and leaves for work and arrives home while he is sleeping. Marcela's mother looks after him, but she worries about their safety, especially after receiving threats from FCROC employees targeting her and her family.

What is your family like?

Marcela I live with my mother and my son. My sister lives with her husband and son in Florida. The father of my son is not involved in Luis's life. It's not because I wanted it that way but because he never took interest. He lives in Chietla but did not ask about his son until Luis

was already two. My mother worries about me because I come home late from SITEKIM meetings and organizing, but she supports what I am doing, which helps me a lot. Once someone from church asked my mom how she could let me go around organizing. My mom responded by saying that the Bible doesn't say it's wrong to organize people, especially if it is to help their situation.

How did you become a union organizer?

It first started because the conditions in Kukdong were bad. They were serving us spoiled and dirty food in the cafeteria. There was a day when the majority of the workers were sick with dysentery. So the supervisors from each sewing line got together and decided to address these problems. Some time after that, they called some of us in to the main office, the ones that the FCROC representative said were the main troublemakers, and tried to force us to sign resignation letters that they had typed up for us, but we refused. Instead they fired us. That's when the workers collectively decided to have a work stoppage in objection to our dismissal.

During the work stoppage workers were beaten up and many were fired. However, because of the media and international attention to the situation, most of us were rehired. But the conditions in the factory have not improved.

A group of workers, through the help of Centro de Apoyo al Trabajador [an NGO founded by USAS activists and local labor activists], decided that the way to bring real change to the factory is to have an independent union represented by workers in the factory rather than FCROC. Since then, that's what we have been trying to do.

Have you worked in any other maquilas?

Before working at Kukdong, I worked in Matamoros Garment. It was horrible there. The union that supposedly represented the workers was also FCROC. We were never paid on time and we were forced to work overtime if we did not finish our daily quota. Even though sign-out was at 6 p.m., we would have to work until after 11 p.m. I guess the reason why the workers in Matamoros Garment never had a work stoppage in protest of the work conditions is because, unlike in Kukdong, the workers were divided. The workers were either scared of losing their jobs or they were, in one way or another, affiliated with FCROC. The conditions got so bad that I decided to leave and work at Kukdong.

What have you learned from your experience?

I realize that the future of democracy in Mexico is in the unionization of workers in maquiladoras. SITEKIM is an example of how a union can function by workers.

Camelia, Elizabet, and Benita Cazales Duarte, Sewing lines 2 and 3, San Francisco Huilango

About an hour from the Kukdong factory there's a small village called Huilango that creeps up the side of a mountain and overlooks miles of fields of avocado, beans, corn and coffee. One phone serves the entire pueblo and the bus only comes every hour and a few times on Sunday. Here the Cazales family has lived for generations. Now eleven people live in the family home. The four oldest children work at Kukdong during the week and help their father in the campo on the weekends. Camelia, twenty-three, Elizabet, nineteen, and Benita, sixteen, work in sewing and their brother, Arsenio, twenty-one, works as a cutter. They rise early Monday morning to take the company bus to work and return late Monday evening only to do it again the next day.

Why did you decide to work in a maquila?

Camelia   After I finished middle school there were only two options for me, to work in the campo or in a maquila, and I didn't want to work in the campo. After four months at my first maquila job, the factory closed. I quickly found work at Kukdong through a bulletin soliciting employees.

Why did you participate in the work stoppage?

Camelia   We wanted things at Kukdong to change. We were protesting the working conditions, the treatment by supervisors, the low salary, and the inedible food.

Do you support SITEKIM?

Benita   SITEKIM will make things better. They support us whereas the FCROC doesn't. If I have a problem I go to Josefina [SITEKIM committee member] because I have confidence in her. She is able to explain the situation and tell me what I have to do. With SITEKIM we will be able to raise our salaries and improve the food.

Elizabet   I think the majority of workers support SITEKIM, but many are afraid of losing their jobs if they affiliate with the independent union. The FCROC threatened that its supporters would throw hot water on independent union members. The FCROC has also been scaring workers by circulating leaflets that say the factory will close if you support SITEKIM. They pay people 100 pesos to support the FCROC and they paid five of their supporters to beat up two SITEKIM members and in the end only the SITEKIM members were suspended from work.

How is the situation in the maquila now?

Elizabet   Right now there isn't a lot of work at the factory. The Korean supervisors treat us better. Before the work stoppage they would yell and scream and hit and kick us in front of all the other workers when something went wrong. They still scream at us, but less than before.

Camelia   The food is also better and cleaner. Before, a lot of our friends were sick with dysentery. Now they give us 70 pesos a week to buy food, but that's only enough to buy a little bit of lunch for the week. Maybe it's because we are from the campo and are used to eating more, but we are always still hungry after lunch.

Elizabet   The FCROC is still robbing 4 pesos from us every week for our dues. We were forced to affiliate with FCROC when we started working at Kukdong. My brother never affiliated yet they still take 4 pesos from his paycheck every week.

Suspended for three days for passing out independent union literature inside the Kukdong factory, Ivánde Erik Díaz Xollo reads over the labor laws in front of the maquila

Benita   None of us likes the security guards. We hope that Alberto Sedano, the head of security, gets fired because he demands that the guards thoroughly check the women workers the four times we enter and leave the factory. It's humiliating. They lift our shirts, look inside our bras and touch our butts. All they do is pat the men down.

Camelia   There are still many discrepancies in workers' salaries. My sister Benita and I make the same, 48 pesos every day, but she started working almost a year after me.

Other people in our line make 10 pesos more than us and we don't know why. Also my paycheck is 363 pesos after taxes including a 37 peso bonus for meeting the quota for the week. But at the bottom of my paycheck 37 pesos are subtracted in pencil, so I earn 326 pesos per week. I don't understand why this happens, but there is no one to ask.

"A real international strategy"

Through visits to garment factories overseas, USAS has been developing contacts with workers and their advocates for several years, and the Kukdong victory shows that such contact can have profound political consequences. Each delegation is different. But generally, the students meet with workers, visit factories (if they're allowed inside), and network with local NGOs. There are usually several bilingual people leading the delegation, along with people who are well-acquainted with the area.

In 1998, in cooperation with the National Labor Committee, student anti-sweatshop activists visited El Salvador, Nicaragua, and Honduras. With help from the National Labor Committee, the students who participated in this week-long delegation produced a report, titled *Behind Closed Doors*. Later, in September 1999, the National Labor Committee took another delegation of students to El Salvador. *Something to Hide*, an educational video put out by the National Labor Committee, documents this delegation.

Jeff Ballinger, of the anti-Nike group Press for Change, sponsored a seven-day delegation to Jakarta, Indonesia, in September 1999. USAS activists Maria Roeper and Molly McGrath visited several factories, networked with various NGOs, and interviewed workers in their homes.

With the help of UNITE, USAS sent three organizers to the Dominican Republic in the spring of 2000. Among the USAS activists who participated in this delegation was David Alvarado, now an organizer in Mexico, whose work has been central to the struggle at the Kukdong factory.

The summer of 2000 was the beginning of the Collegiate Apparel Research Initiative (CARI). CARI delegations are longer, more intensive, data-collecting projects than USAS's previous, week-long delegations. On CARI's month-long trips, USAS activists collect data, and meet with workers, local NGOs, union officials, and students. USAS activists began CARI so they could better understand garment workers' struggles and the local contexts in which they take place. Each of these trips produces a report, intended to inform organizing by USAS and other anti-sweatshop groups.

USAS sent organizers to Mexico City with the United Electrical Workers (UE) in November 2000. In Mexico, USAS activists Eric Brakken, Evelyn Zepeda, Molly McGrath, and David Alvarado met with a Kukdong worker just as their struggle was beginning, and had conversations that laid the groundwork for later solidarity. This delegation took place in coordination with the AFL–CIO Solidarity Center in Mexico City and the Frente Autentico del Trabajo (FAT), UE's sister union in Mexico.

The most important solidarity visit USAS has initiated to date was in spring 2001, when USAS sent its own delegation to Atlixco de Puebla, Mexico. Seventeen USAS activists met with the Kukdong union leaders and brainstormed ways for the student movement to keep pressure on the Nike Corporation and on their universities. The students also went to the workers' neighborhoods and visited them in their homes to let them know there was solidarity work going on in the US. One day, students went to the factory before the work shift started one morning and leafletted outside to show the workers their support for the union.

Students also hung out with the Kukdong workers, playing soccer and going out dancing. Adam Szlachetka, an activist from Michigan State University, said of the Kukdong workers: "They were all just normal kids like us – a lot of them were younger than us – and really gave us a whole different view on the struggle. We realized we were working with people who were a lot like our friends back home."

In March 2001, a delegation visited the New Era factory near Buffalo, New York, and in the summer of 2001 USAS again organized CARI delegations to Indonesia, Honduras, and Mexico.

Molly McGrath

nine

Beyond the horror stories: fighting everyday inequality

Liana Molina grew up in El Paso, not far from the maquiladoras and the grinding poverty of Juarez. "You see women and children begging everywhere," she says. But her experience is unusual: most USAS activists grew up nowhere near a sweatshop. In fact, they are an unusually privileged group of people. The movement began at the country's most monied universities – in a recent front-page story, even the *Wall Street Journal*, a close observer of the ruling class, marvelled at the extraordinary affluence of the student body at Duke, one of the schools where USAS began. In a 1999 survey for a paper by economists Richard Freeman and Kimberly Ann Elliott, researcher Peter Siu found that over a third of the USAS activists reported a family income of over $100,000, more than twice the proportion of all first-year college students with that family income. Only 8 percent of USAS activists reported a family income of less than $40,000, compared to 35 percent of first-year college students. That survey is dated, especially since USAS now has chapters at many public schools, from Western Michigan University to Georgia State, and is expanding its efforts to recruit students in community colleges and other state institutions. But there's no doubt that USAS still represents an unusually affluent group.

No historian of student activism would be surprised by this. There are always exceptions, but since its twelfth-century beginnings, the history of student activism has generally been one of intra-elite struggle. As Mark Boren points out in *Student Resistance: A History of the Unruly Subject*, universities themselves were begun by students, "the sons of the well-to-do and rising middle class," not for the pursuit of knowledge but "for the express purpose of wielding economic power and for generating financial leverage against host towns and cities." In 1200, for instance, the University of Paris, which at that time was a collective of students, threatened to withdraw from the city and extorted substantial legal and economic concessions from it. Centuries later, of course, the Port Huron statement made its authors' privilege explicit: "We are people of this generation, bred in at least modest comfort." Student activists use their own elite status to influence other elites (school administrators, CEOs, national governments), and some of their power lies in that fact. Students, especially those at upper-class institutions, can attract attention from and wield influence upon elites in a way that many ordinary people can't.

Given its members' affluence, USAS represents an unusual brand of labor activism. Like contemporary feminism, the labor movement has emphasized self-determination, and although affluent ladies did agitate on behalf of garment workers at the turn of the last century, large-scale mobilizations over the labor of others have been relatively rare in history. Because it is not focused on the activists' own labor, the student anti-sweatshop movement is not, in itself, a labor movement. Indeed, at least in its beginnings, it was a movement premissed on the activists' class privilege. It is worth considering the implications of that paradox.

The sweatshop issue is, in a sense, a natural one for affluent students. Like many First World anti-sweatshop campaigns, the student movement arose in part out of a sense of privilege. The group was born in a period of economic prosperity, when affluent students were feeling unusually fortunate, and less worried about their careers than their predecessors in the jobless early 1990s. USAS activists attend schools whose logos convey prestige, a prestige worth defending. While less affluent students are more likely to organize on their own behalf, against tuition hikes or campus racism, upper-middle-class white students have the luxury of organizing against their own privilege. Ironically, that sort of radicalism can be challenging for working-class students, who may feel they're in college not to critique privilege, but to court it. "All these problems are caused by an elite, yet we're striving to be part of that elite," says Liana Molina. "I came [to school] to get a degree, to get a better job."

The effectiveness of the larger student movement will depend on building coalitions across such differences, and USAS is already making great strides toward cross-class solidarity by working with unions, and with low-wage workers on their campuses. Initially, the movement was driven less by that sort of solidarity than by students' sense of distance between the sweatshop and their own world, a world of calm, leafy campuses and well-stocked shopping malls. Some enter the movement believing the sweatshop an aberration in a system that otherwise works well. Though USAS's public face can look quite confrontational – students occupying administration buildings and denouncing neoliberal economics – not all students come to anti-sweatshop activism with a militant outlook. One Penn freshman, a USAS member who participated in a February 2000 sit-in, earnestly described himself as a "capitalist." Few would go that far in their enthusiasm for the current economic and social arrangements, but in interviews, countless USAS activists, usually early on in their activism, have been quick to point out that opposition to sweatshops was "not that radical."

In a sense, they are right. Sweatshops viscerally outrage mainstream America in a way that the routine exploitation of workers employed in the legal low-wage sector does not. Andrew Ross concludes his 1997 book *No Sweat: Fashion, Free Trade and the Rights of Garment Workers* by observing a "conceptual problem" with anti-sweatshop activism:

> the growing tendency to see sweatshops, however defined, as an especially abhorrent species of labor, and therefore in a moral class of their own ... apart from the lawful low-wage sector, which is condoned as a result. .. The fact is that virtually every low-wage job ... fails to provide an adequate standard of living.... Installing proper fire exits may turn a sweatshop into a legal workplace, but it remains a low-wage atrocity.

Ross underscores the importance of re-defining

> "sweatshop" as a general description of all exploitive labor conditions.... Given its powerful associations with inhumane and immoral treatment, and given its current visibility, the garment sweatshop may be poised ... to serve as the crusading vector for the labor movement as a whole.

No Sweat was published the same year that anti-sweatshop activism hit the US campus. Rather than rationalizing routine exploitation, as Ross feared, the movement seems to have radicalized people in exactly the way he hoped. "People are drawn in [to anti-sweatshop activism] by the horror stories," says the WRC's Maria Roeper, "but then they start seeing how the whole system works."

USAS politicizes students' humanitarian impulses. There are always students with a social conscience, who are concerned about the suffering of the poor. They volunteer in soup kitchens; some even join the Peace Corps after graduation. But in the absence of any larger activist movement, they are often powerless to fight the political and economic inequalities that cause suffering. Anti-sweatshop activism attracts many of the students of conscience that would, in less political times, be drawn to volunteer work, and teaches them something they might not have expected to learn. Learning to think about the "whole system," to connect the sweatshop to drilling in the Arctic Circle and privatization of education, students realize that they don't just want to "help" the less fortunate, but to live in a better, more democratic world. An "Aboriginal sister," quoted on USAS's website, puts it best: "If you have come to help me, you are wasting your time. But if you've come because your liberation is bound up with mine, then let us work together."

USAS involvement is thus a stepping stone – or, as many students joke, a "gateway drug" – to an awareness of the exploitation in all low-wage jobs, and to labor activism at home. "If I hadn't gotten involved in the sweatshop struggle I probably wouldn't have got involved in the [campus] labor issue," says James Nussbaumer, a student at the University of Southern California. Indeed, students at the University of Tennessee, Earlham in Indiana, the University of Wisconsin, Ohio State, University of Connecticut, and numerous other institutions have been fighting for better wages and work conditions for campus workers, often helping in their union drives and working closely with them. (This sort of work actually predates USAS – the first Student Labor Action Committee was established in 1994, to support locked-out workers at the A.E. Staley Company in Decatur, Illinois – but USAS has nourished it immeasurably, raising student consciousness about labor rights, and providing both networks and momentum.) At Wesleyan, Johns Hopkins, Harvard, University of Connecticut and elsewhere, students have staged sit-ins to urge their university administrations to stop tolerating such contractors' exploitation of workers on campus, and to pressure those companies to recognize worker-organized unions. (Students objected to illegal union-busting practices, and the failure to pay workers a living wage, among other abuses.) Of these, Wesleyan's occupation was perhaps the most successful; the administration ended up agreeing to better wages, benefits, and job security for the janitors.

Part of the reason for this evolution is that the organization has moved, students say, through its partnerships with workers, from a focus on codes of conduct to an awareness that there is no substitute for workers' own organizing efforts. Though many unions are seriously flawed in practice, no code can take the place of union representation. At the time of writing, USAS's major campaigns lend support to worker-led struggles in the United States and abroad, and it is unlikely that this emphasis will change.

USAS has built strong relationships with North American unions, which are, in turn, showing remarkable dedication to the new generation. The AFL–CIO contributed some $40,000 to USAS in academic year 1999–2000, and some $50,000 the following year. Many students are taking jobs as union organizers not only during the summer but also upon graduation. (Veterans of anti-campaigns also go to work for groups like STITCH and the National Labor Committee.) This postgraduate labor activism has another great advantage: it keeps veterans involved in the student movement, as they are frequently hired to coordinated student/labor alliances. Turnover is one of student activism's biggest curses, and struggles entirely confined to campus usually peter out fairly quickly, precisely because there's no way to keep graduates involved. USAS's strong relationship with US unions is helping the organization build domestic solidarity, and suggests that the group won't dissolve after a few significant triumphs, as the 1980s' anti-apartheid movement did.

Though unions are rightly criticized for hiring these outside organizers rather than training people from within the rank and file, there's no doubt that the graduates of the student movement are invigorating unions. Dave Snyder, one of the activists who organized the Johns Hopkins living-wage sit-in and is now an organizer with HERE, has been pushing his local to work with Jobs with Justice, and to participate in global anti-corporate events like the April 2001 anti-FTAA protests in Quebec City. "I have to humble myself, and stop some of these grandiose ideas," he admits, explaining that his efforts aren't always successful. "But I do think that students can bring their radicalism into the labor movement."

USAS's 2001 summer conference, at Chicago's Loyola University, passed a resolution redefining the organization's own mission, making explicit what had been a reality for some time: USAS is now a broad-based student labor solidarity group, no longer exclusively focused on garment exploitation in the Third World. Though some observers worry that the organization is spreading itself too thin, it is a welcome evolution given the urgency of economic inequality in students' backyards, and the power they have, both to bring about small but significant reforms, and to shape public consciousness. To that latter end, agitation from elite students is crucial, but USAS's work with US workers, and its attempts to build a more working-class student constituency, will prove equally vital.

Is USAS here to stay? It's difficult to say, given the volatile state of both the left and the larger world, and the ever-changing nature of student activism. But Jackie Bray, who as a sophomore is a relative youngster in the organization's national leadership, is hopeful. She and her fellow activists have been working hard to recruit younger members to ensure the organization's longevity; recently, a number of high schools have established USAS chapters. After a long conversation praising her older USAS role models – especially "mentor" Laura McSpedon, a founding USAS member who now works for Jobs With Justice – she says, "I hope in four years you'll be talking to some first-year student, and she'll say 'Oh yeah, Jackie Bray. She was OK. But what we're doing works even better.'"

Harvard versus Harvard: a community fights a corporation

After we had been sitting in the president's office for a week, the dining hall workers came. Exhausted from the tensest week of my life, I was sitting at a beautifully polished antique wood table, staring at the president's complete twenty-volume collection of "The Tanner Lectures on Human Values" when I first heard them. Many dining hall workers had visited us before, but suddenly there were hundreds of them, roaring their support for those of us inside. In identical red sweatshirts that proclaimed "Never Surrender," they surrounded the building, electrifying Harvard Yard. Residents of the freshman dorms and of the tent city that had sprung up to support our sit-in streamed out to join them, and soon more than five hundred people had gathered in the middle of Massachusetts Avenue at 10 p.m. to demand a living wage for all Harvard employees.

The forty students occupying Massachusetts Hall, which houses the offices of Harvard's president, provost and treasurer, could not join them there, of course, but neither could we have been happier to see them. Our sit-in was the culmination of a three-year organizing campaign for a living wage for all Harvard

employees, and now the entire Harvard community had joined us in this demand.

This sit-in embodies the conflict between Harvard the community and Harvard the corporation. On the one hand, Harvard wants to foster "genuinely free and responsible discussion" (as the president wrote in a statement criticizing our action). On the other, Harvard pays more than a thousand workers poverty wages while sitting atop an endowment of almost $20 billion. Janitors, security guards, and dining hall workers earn as little as $6.75 an hour and work up to ninety hours a week. Our Living Wage Campaign demands that Harvard implement a minimum $10.25 per hour wage with benefits, the same standard enacted by the Cambridge City Council in 1998. Hundreds of Harvard employees work two and even three jobs and still struggle to support their families. As a custodian said, "Look, this is not a matter of working hard – people are already working hard. I've been wearing a custodial uniform now going on twenty years. I always say the only thing we don't have is a number across our backs. They figure they own me like a piece of equipment – like a barrel or a buffing machine."

Five of the six members of the Harvard Corporation, the University's highest governing board, are out-of-state millionaires who jet in for meetings. Robert Stone, chairman of the search committee that selected Lawrence Summers as Harvard's next president, is long-time commodore of the New York Yacht Club. Herbert Winokur is a director of Enron, a destructive global energy giant and George W. Bush's biggest corporate backer [a name now synonymous with corporate corruption and the all-too-cozy relations between politicians and corporations]. D. Ronald Daniel is the director of McKinsey & Co. (and quite a golf fan, if the portraits of rich sportsmen in his plush office here are any guide). These people have the final say over everything at Harvard, from the janitors to the endowment to tenure.

For three years the administration refused any meaningful dialogue or action on the living wage. In fact, since we began the campaign Harvard has outsourced and cut wages and benefits for hundreds more workers. Because things were getting worse and the administration refused even to talk, a sit-in became necessary.

As I write, we have occupied the offices of the president, provost, and treasurer of Harvard for about two weeks. We've been sleeping on their Persian rugs, sitting in their antique chairs and redecorating their walls

with our "Workers Can't Eat Prestige" posters (using university-approved poster tacks, of course). We are deeply gratified by the incredible things happening outside. Harvard Yard has mutated from a staid pastoral setting into a massive tent city of supporters so densely populated that there is a waiting list to sleep out. More than four hundred members of Harvard's famously atomistic faculty have signed a petition and took out a full-page ad in the Boston Globe. Alumni have started a fund for the Harvard Workers Center, a law-student-run group that provides free legal support to Harvard's workers. Five US senators and four representatives have pledged their support. Former Labor Secretary Robert Reich and AFL–CIO president John Sweeney have come to the steps of Massachusetts Hall to demand justice for Harvard's workers. Our rallies have swelled to almost two thousand people – more than have gathered for a cause in Harvard Yard in decades.

But most important has been the total transformation of the role of workers on campus. The more than a thousand workers who receive poverty wages have long been scared even to speak with members of the campaign for fear of being fired. Now, security guards denounce poverty wages in fiery speeches on the steps of the president's office and custodians organize marches across campus to demand decent wages. And as I write, hundreds of dining hall workers are coming back to Mass Hall to demand a living wage and to celebrate our two solid weeks of occupying the offices of the people who thought they could block the consensus of an entire community.

Benjamin L. McKean

Coda

The victory at Kukdong was the campus anti-sweatshop movement's most substantial yet. In early September 2001, USAS activists all over the United States received word of the union's recognition, and cheered it, knowing that although it was first and foremost a workers' victory, their own role had been considerable and historic. Meanwhile, students were launching organizing campaigns to support the New Era workers, who went on strike that same month. The global economic justice movement proceeded apace: many USAS activists were preparing to go to Washington DC to protest at the IMF/World Bank meetings on September 30.

On September 11, 2001, as we all know, thousands of lives were shattered, and the global political landscape was altered in ways that may take years to comprehend fully. At first, many activists feared that North America's burgeoning anticorporate movement – indeed, all emerging forms of political dissent – will become a casualty of the terrorists. The September 30 IMF/World Bank meetings – for which Washington DC police had expected some fifty thousand demonstrators, from the controversial hooded Anti-Capitalist Convergence (or "Black Bloc") to the AFL–CIO – were cancelled. Most protest groups cancelled their actions too, and not only because there were no meetings to oppose. At a moment of sorrow and panic, demonstrators risked being ignored – or, worse, reviled as unpatriotic or insensitive to the memories of the dead. In a statement explaining their withdrawal from the protests, USAS declared September in the capital "neither the time nor the place to gather in opposition."

Still, a few weeks later, USAS resumed work on the New Era campaign, still buoyed by the Kukdong triumph. New institutions continued to join the WRC, and in November students' spirits were lifted by learning that workers had voted to unionize at BJ&B, a factory in the Dominican Republic that makes baseball caps for many USAS schools. USAS had been supporting this campaign for years – one of the organization's earliest efforts at cross-border solidarity – so the victory was a profound one. As the response of the United States government to the September 11 attacks grew more brutal, many students threw themselves into anti-war organizing. Groups like USAS had established such strong left student networks – and created such a ready culture of dissent – that anti-war protest was visible on many campuses before the bombs even started falling. The new peace activism, which had by late November 2001 touched at least four hundred campuses nationwide, has an even more visceral appeal than the anti-sweatshop movement. It is attracting a wider range of students, including rural, Southern schools (North Carolina's Appalachia State and the University of Southern Mississippi), historically black colleges like Morehouse, community colleges from Boston to Hawaii, urban public universities like the University of Illinois–Chicago and CUNY, high schools and middle schools. A newly formed National Youth and Student Peace and Justice Coalition will startle anyone who imagines that all peace activists are white folk-music fans; in addition to groups like USAS, it includes the youth division of the Black Radical Congress and the Muslim Student Association. Many USAS activists see the emerging anti-war movement as an opportunity for a much larger student movement to emerge, one that looks a lot more like America's economically, regionally, and racially varied society.

USAS and the larger student movement face some challenges. Prolonged war – and anti-war activism – could test the warm solidarity developed in recent years between students and labor, though students and workers alike have been working hard to prevent that. There's also the problem of finite human resources: the student movement accomplishes a lot with only a handful of core activists, and sustained opposition to war – important as that is – could drain activist attention from labor issues. That's why, Jackie Bray says, "There is absolute consensus in the organization that we're sticking with labor." USAS endorses peace organizing and is part of the emerging student "peace and justice movment," but feels strongly that its strength lies in its ties to the labor movement. Says Rachel Edelman, a recent University of Michigan graduate who now works full-time in the USAS office, "It is more important than ever to fight in solidarity with workers, given the conservative backlash, and the fact that so many workers are losing their jobs."

On the other hand, it may be difficult to help garment workers win victories, as that industry is in the midst of a global slowdown. Garment workers all over the world risk losing their jobs as factories get fewer orders; that's not a good climate for organizing. There's also a danger that recession may leave students too anxious about their own futures to organize. The triple extremities of war, terror, and recession could distract the public from capitalism's everyday inequities. On the other hand, they certainly dramatize the system's problems: Bush's tax breaks to corporations; the way every national burden, from economic slowdown to anthrax, is disproportionately shouldered by the working class. USAS activists see tremendous opportunity in this moment.

Many activists say that the September 11 attacks have left people ever hungrier for forward-looking, optimistic social action. The global economic justice movement in particular may stand a better chance of being heard, at a time when Americans are suddenly looking at the rest of the world and wondering, "Why do 'they' hate us?" Says Jackie Bray, "People are beginning to ask questions." For many, September 11 underscored the need to rethink America's role in the world, and to redress global economic inequality. It is in this spirit that USAS continues to move forward. As the organization asserted in its post-September 11 statement, "We realize that there is a great deal of work and healing ahead of us, and hope to move forward from this moment to build a more just and inclusive place."

Timeline

1980s	Garment industry workers in the global South, as well as immigrant women in the United States, begin organizing for better wages and work conditions.
1990	Laid-off Levi Strauss & Co. workers in San Antonio, Texas, launch a national boycott of the company, demanding a severance package and retraining, and carry out hunger strikes and pickets.
	The National Labor Committee (NLC) adopts sweatshops as its signature issue.
	The Clean Clothes Campaign begins in the Netherlands.
1992	Activist Jeff Ballinger begins a campaign to expose Nike's abusive labor practices in Indonesia. Other anti-sweatshop campaigns emerge, also focusing on Nike.
1994	The first Student Labor Action Coalition (SLAC) developed at the University of Wisconsin–Madison, to support 700 workers who were locked out at the A.E. Staley Company in Decatur, Illinois.
1995	Sweatshop Watch forms in California, in response to the discovery that an El Monte sweatshop uses forced labor.
Mid-1990s	More SLACs emerge.
	Graduate student employees begin to organize unions.
	UNITE runs a campaign focusing on the labor conditions of Guess Jeans workers.

1996	Clinton adminstration establishes the Fair Labor Association (FLA).
Spring 1996	Charlie Kernaghan of the NLC makes Kathie Lee Gifford cry.
Summer 1996	AFL–CIO's Union Summer internship program begins.
Fall 1996	Over 200 student labor activists gather in Madison, Wisconsin, for the Youth-in-Action Conference.
1997	Duke students campaign for a code of conduct and win. Other students begin similar campaigns.
1998	Several labor unions and religious groups resign from the FLA, objecting to the excessive influence of its corporate members.
Spring 1998	USAS is formally established.
1999	Students nationwide continue to negotiate with administrators over codes of conduct.
	Students at Duke, Georgetown, and universities of Arizona, Michigan and North Carolina-Chapel Hill occupy administrators' offices, forcing their institutions to commit to full disclosure of licensees' factory locations.
	University of Wisconsin–Madison commits to a study of the living wage issue.
November 1999	Thousands protest against the World Trade Organization in Seattle, bringing the anticorporate globalization movement to North America.
February 2000	University of Pennsylvania students occupy their president's office, demanding that the school withdraw from the FLA and join a new organization free of corporate influence, the Worker Rights Consortium (WRC).
Spring 2000	Students at the universities of Michigan, Wisconsin, Oregon, Iowa, and Kentucky, as well as SUNY–Albany, Tulane, Purdue and Macalester hold sit-ins, making the same demand.
	Purdue students hold an eleven-day hunger strike, also urging WRC membership.

Students at Johns Hopkins and Wesleyan hold sit-ins over campus workers' wages and work conditions.

Nike cancels its contract with Brown University, upset at the institution's membership of the WRC.

Students travel to the Dominican Republic to investigate a Nike supplier which made University of Michigan hats, where workers were being fired for attempting to organize unions.

April 2000   The WRC holds its founding meeting, boasting nearly 50 collegiate members.

The entire ten-school University of California system joins the organization.

Thousands gather in Washington DC to protest the IMF/ World Bank meetings.

Students begin a campaign to pressure Sodexho-Marriott, a campus dining service provider, to divest from private prisons.

Nike broke with the University of Michigan – by far its biggest collegiate contract – after UM joined the WRC.

Mad about the school's WRC membership, Phil Knight withdraws a $30 million gift to the University of Oregon.

Summer 2000   Ten students, along with fired Dominican garment worker Roselio Reyes, launch the "Nike Truth Tour," protesting at Niketown stores from New York City to Chicago to Las Vegas and finally Eugene, Oregon.

At its national conference, USAS faces conflicts over organizational structure.

Fall 2000   USAS organization adopts more radical Principles of Unity, stating that sweatshops are a symptom of larger problems in the global economy and that the struggle for workers' rights is tied to struggles against racism, sexism, homophopia, and all other forms of oppression. The organization adopts a more viable structure.

January 2001   Nike and University of Wisconsin–Madison kiss and make up, signing a seven-year deal, in which Nike will outfit all

UM's varsity teams, and pay $1.2 million annually for the rights to the school's logo.

Workers go on strike at the Kukdong factory in Atlixco de Puebla, Mexico, which makes sweatshirts for many major US universities. The workers involved are fired.

Students begin a campaign to pressure administrators and manufacturers to force the factory to rehire the Kukdong workers, improve wages and conditions and recognize their independent union.

April 2001	Thousands protest against the FTAA meeting in Quebec City.
Spring 2001	Hundreds of Penn State students camp out in the student union for nine days, protesting the university's failure to respond to racist death threats against black students.
Summer 2001	USAS redefines itself as a student/labor solidarity organization, still committed to overseas garment industry workers, but also to using their power in labor struggles closer to home.
September 2001	Kukdong workers win recognition for independent union, as a result of USAS and WRC pressure.
	Anti-war organizing begins on campuses nationwide.
	USAS begins campus campaigns in solidarity with striking workers at the New Era factory in Buffalo, who make hats for many Big Ten universities.
November/ December 2001	Kukdong (now Mexmode) workers tour US campuses nationwide to celebrate victory and raise awareness about student power and international solidarity.

Laura McSpedon contributed
to this timeline

Sources

introduction

United States General Accounting Office. "Garment Industry: Efforts to Address the Prevalence and Conditions of Sweatshops," HEHS-95-29. Washington DC, November 2, 1994.

International Communications Research (ICR). "The Consumer and Sweatshops," Marymount University Center for Ethical Concerns, Arlington VA, 1999.

one

Arnold, Wayne, "The A.F.L.–C.I.O. Organizes in Cambodia," *New York Times*, July 12, 2001.

Benjamin, Medea. "Toil and Trouble: Student Activism in the Fight Against Sweatshops." In *Campus, Inc.: Corporate Power in the Ivory Tower*, ed. Geoffrey White with Flannery C. Hauck, Prometheus, Amherst NY, 2000.

Cooper, Marc. "No Sweat: Uniting Workers and Students, A New Movement is Born," *Nation*, June 7, 1999.

Greenhouse, Steven. "A Crusader Makes Celebrities Tremble," *New York Times*, June 18, 1996.

Louie, Miriam Ching Yoon. *Sweatshop Warriors, Immigrant Women Take on the Global Factory*, South End Press, Cambridge MA, 2001.

Ross, Andrew, ed. *No Sweat: Fashion, Free Trade and the Rights of Garment Workers*, Verso, London and New York, 1997.

two

Portions of this chapter appeared in Liza Featherstone's "The New Student Movement," *The Nation*, May 15, 2000.

Worker Rights Consortium: www.workersrights.org.

Fair Labor Association: fairlabor.org.

three

Portions of this chapter appeared in Liza Featherstone's "The New Student Movement," *Nation*, May 15, 2000; "The Student Movement Comes of Age," *Nation*, October 16, 2000, and "A Common Enemy: Students Fight Private Prisons," *Dissent*, Fall 2000.

Bourdieu, Pierre, *Acts of Resistance*, The New Press, New York, 1988. See especially "The Left Hand and the Right Hand of the State," interview first published in *Le Monde*, January 14, 1992.

Cleaver, Harry. *Reading "Capital" Politically*, University of Texas Press, Austin, 1979.

Henwood, Doug. *A New Economy?* Verso, New York, 2002.

Henwood, Doug. *Wall Street: How it Works and for Whom*, Verso, New York, 1997.

Klein, Naomi. *No Logo: Taking Aim at the Brand Bullies*, Picador, New York, 2000.

Parenti, Christian. *Lockdown America*, Verso, New York, 1999.

Students for a Democratic Society. "The Port Huron Statement of the Students for a Democratic Society," Students for a Democratic Society, New York, June 15, 1962.

four

Passages in this chapter are lifted from an article Liza Featherstone co-authored with Doug Henwood, "Clothes Encounters: Economists and Activists Clash Over Sweatshops," *Lingua Franca*, March 2001.

Academic Consortium on International Trade. "Letter to University Presidents," drafted July 2000, sent September 25, 2000. www.spp.umich.edu/rsie/acit/.

Bhagwati, Jagdish. "Why Nike is on the Right Track," longer version of an editorial published in the *Financial Times*, May 1, 2000.

Emerson, Tony. "Swoosh Wars: In an Operation Modeled on the Clinton Campaign Machine, Nike Takes On its Enemies," *Newsweek*, March 12, 2001.

Featherstone, Liza and Doug Henwood. "Economists vs. Students," *Nation*, February 12, 2001.

Global Alliance for Workers and Communities, "Workers' Voices," February 2001. www.theglobalalliance.org.

Kristof, Nicholas D. and Sheryl WuDunn. "Two Cheers for Sweatshops," *New York Times Magazine*, September 24, 2000.

Nike: www.nikebiz.com.

Scholars Against Sweatshop Labor (SASL). "Statement," October 22, 2001.

five

Portions of this chapter are lifted from Liza Featherstone's "The Student Movement Comes of Age," *Nation*, October 16, 2000.

Di Franco, Ani. "Dark Coffee." *Ani Di Franco*. Righteous Babe Records, Buffalo, 1992.

Gerlach, Luther and Virginia Hine. *People, Power, Change*, Bobbs Merrill, New York 1970.

Sayres, Sonya, et al., eds. *The 60s Without Apology*, University of Minnesota Press in cooperation with *Social Text*, Minneapolis 1984.

Krouzman, Roni. *Democratic Organizing for a Democratic Society*, unpublished, 1999.

Lappé, Francis Moore. *Rediscovering America's Values*, Ballantine, New York, 1989.

six

Sidebar from the Penn State University Village website: www.geocities.com/psuvillage/.

Larimore-Hall, Daraka, and Tracie McMillan. *The Activist*, Young Democratic Socialists of America, Summer 2001.

seven

Bellafante, Ginia. "Is Feminism Dead?" *Time*, June 29, 1998.

Centro de Apoyo al Trabajador and Collegiate Apparel Research Initiative. *La Luche Sigue: Stories from the People of the Kuk-dong Factory*, July 2001.

Hardt, Michael, and Antonio Negri. *Empire*, Harvard University Press, Cambridge MA, 2000.

Kabeer, Naila. *The Power to Choose: Bangladeshi Women and Labor Market Decisions in London and Dhaka*, Verso, London, 2000.

Mohanty, Chandra Talpade. "Women Workers and Capitalist Scripts: Ideologies of Domination, Common Interests, and the Politics of Solidarity." In *Feminist Genealogies, Colonial Legacies, Democratic Futures*, ed. M. Jacqui Alexander and Chandra Talpade Mohanty, Routledge, New York, 1997.

Pollitt. Katha. "Does Your Generation Resent Up-and-coming Young Women?" In *Letters of Intent: Women Cross the Generations to Talk About Family, Work, Sex, Love and the Future of Feminism*, ed. Anna Bondoc and Meg Daly, The Free Press, New York, 1999.

Traub-Werner, Marion. "Untitled: Sweatshops, Solidarity and Guatemala," undergraduate thesis, unpublished, 1999.

Wilson, Rachel: http://sasua.org/rachelphotos.html.

eight

Portions of this chapter first appeared in a brief item in the *Nation*'s "In Fact" section, written by Liza Featherstone.

The worker interviews previously appeared in Collegiate Apparel Research Initiative. *La Luche Sigue: Stories from the People of the Kuk-dong factory*, July 2001.

Behind Closed Doors: www.nlcnet.org/behindclosed/toc.htm.

Burnett, John. "All Things Considered," National Public Radio, August 14, 2001.

CARI archives: www.behindthelabel.org.

Ponce, Josefina Hernandez. "Mayday Letter of Solidarity from the Kukdong Workers," April 30, 2001.

United Students Against Sweatshops. *Money Made, Workers Forgotten: The Untold Stories of the Global Race to the Bottom in Western New York*, Spring 2001.

Worker Rights Consortium. *WRC Investigation Re: Complaint Against Kukdong (Mexico)*, June 20, 2001.

Worker Rights Consortium. *WRC Investigation Re: Complaint Against Kukdong (Mexico), Preliminary Findings and Recommendations*, January 24, 2001.

Worker Rights Consortium. *WRC Assessment re: Complaint Against New Era Cap Co., Inc., Preliminary Findings and Recommendations*, August 10, 2001.

nine

Benjamin McKean's essay is adapted from two of his previously published editorials: "At Harvard, Living Wage Meets the Ivy League," *Los Angeles Times*, May 6, 2001; and "Harvard's Shame," *Nation*, May 21, 2001.

Boren, Mark Edelman. *Student Resistance: A History of the Unruly Subject*, Routledge, New York, 2001.

Elliott, Kimberley Ann and Richard Freeman. "White Hats or Don Quixotes? Human Rights Vigilantes in the Global Economy," paper for NBER Conference on Emerging Labor Market Institutions, 2000.

Kaufman, Jonathan. "At Elite Universities, a Culture of Money Highlights Class Divide," *Wall Street Journal*, June 8, 2001.

Ross, Andrew, ed. *No Sweat: Fashion, Free Trade and the Rights of Garment Workers*, Verso, New York, 1997.

Ross, Andrew. "Riot Boys and Girls," *Village Voice*, August 8–14, 2001.

Students for a Democratic Society. "The Port Huron Statement of the Students for a Democratic Society," 1962.

coda

Featherstone, Liza. "Students Wrestle with War," *Nation*, December 17, 2001.

United Students Against Sweatshops. "Statement on September 11," September 14, 2001.

United Students Against Sweatshops

It is not possible to get a full list of all the schools where students are running campus anti-sweatshop campaigns. No one knows how many there are. Below is a list of schools where student labor activists are officially affiliated with USAS.

United Students Against Sweatshops (USAS)

888 16th St NW, Suite 303
Washington DC 20006
(202) NO-SWEAT
www.usasnet.org

Midatlantic

American University
Carnegie Mellon University
George Washington University
Georgetown University
Lafayette College
Lehigh University
St. Joseph's University
Susquehanna University
University of Delaware
University of Pennsylvania
University of Pittsburgh
Villanova University
Wheeling Jesuit University

Midwest

Alma College
Central Michigan University
Depauw University
Grand Valley St University
Grinnell College
Indiana University
Kenyon College
Loyola University Chicago
Manchester College
Miami University of Ohio
Michigan State University
Notre Dame University
Ohio State University
Purdue University
St. Mary's College
St. Olaf College
University of Akron
University of Chicago
University of Illinois–Chicago
University of Iowa

University of Michigan–Ann Arbor
University of Missouri–Columbia
University of Northern Iowa
University of Wisconsin–Madison
University of Wisconsin–Steven's
Point
Western Michigan University

Northeast

Bard College
Bates College
Boston University
Brown University
Clark University
Cornell University
Fordham University
Harvard University
Holy Cross College
Middlebury College
Mt. Holyoke College
New York University
Vassar College
University of Connecticut
University of Southern Maine
Yale University

Southeast

Berea College
Duke University
Florida State University
Georgia State University
James Madison University
Rice University
Transylvania University
Trinity University
Tulane University

Virginia Tech
University of Kentucky
University of North Carolina–Chapel
Hill
University of Tennessee–Knoxville
University of Virginia
Washington and Lee

West

New Mexico State University
Northern Arizona University
Seattle University
University of Arizona
University of Oregon
University of Wyoming
Western Oregon

California region

Cal Poly San Luis Obispo
Chico State
Occidental College
Pitzer College
San Diego State University
San Francisco State
San Jose State University
UC Berkeley
UC Santa Barbara
UCLA
University of San Francisco

High-school affiliates

Colton High School (CA)
Bergen Academies (NJ)
Fremd High School (IL)
Sharon High School (MA)
Albuquerque Academy (NM)

Acknowledgements

This book would never have existed without Colin Robinson, Molly McGrath, all the workers, students, and union organizers we ever interviewed, the USAS writers and Betsy Reed of the *Nation* magazine. To Rachel Edelman, Doug Henwood, Kitty Krupat, Karen Miller, Andrew Ross, and Evelyn Zepeda, immeasurable gratitude for reading drafts of this manuscript, and for providing kind yet fiercely intelligent feedback. Profound thanks, too, to Anne-Marie Cusac, Rachel Neumann, Matt Rothschild, Laura Secor, Alex Star, and Katrina vanden Heuvel, all of whom edited material that eventually ended up in this book. The Nation Institute funded much of this book's research and for that deserves tremendous props.

Picture credits

The photographs on pages 3, 5, 15, 39, 49, 57, 77 and 85 are by Chad Sullivan; on page 23 by Molly McGrath; on page 60 by Dan Lutz; and on page 89 by Bennett James Baumer. The author and publishers are grateful for permission to reproduce them here.

Notes on contributors

Liza Featherstone is a journalist who writes frequently about student and youth activism. She has contributed to the *Nation, New York Times, Washington Post, Newsday, Ms., Rolling Stone, Lingua Franca, Left Business Observer, In These Times, San Francisco Bay Guardian, Dissent, Sydney Morning Herald, Boston Phoenix, Salon, Nerve, Alternet* and *Columbia Journalism Review*, among other publications. She lives in New York City.

In 1999, **Tico Almeida** graduated from Duke University. He spent the year 2000 as a Fulbright Scholar in South America, where he studied proposals to link core labor standards to the MERCOSUR trade agreement between Argentina, Brazil, Paraguay, and Uruguay. He then handled international labor rights and trade issues for Congressman George Miller's (D-CA) US House Education and Workforce Committee staff. Tico is now a student at Yale Law School.

David Alvarado was born in Mexico City in 1977. In 1997 he moved to the United States with his family, and became a student in the Music School of the University of Wisconsin–Madison for a year. There he became involved with the campus anti-sweatshop group. He returned to Mexico in 2000, and is now working with Centro de Apoyo al Trabajador (CAT), a new NGO that acts as a resource for workers seeking to have their labor rights respected in the state of Puebla. He was instrumental in establishing the close relationship between USAS and the Kukdong workers.

Bennett James Baumer is a senior at Indiana University, studying philosophy and political science. He is twenty-two years old and was born in Wayne County, Indiana, near the town of Centerville. Both of his parents are unionists, members of the Indiana State Teachers Association (NEA), and his extended family boasts other union members and farmers. This past year he studied in La Universidad Complutense Madrid where he was involved with Movimiento de Resistancia Global Madrid and other activist groups. He also attended the International Clean Clothes Campaign conference in Barcelona, where he began a relationship with the Spanish Clean Clothes Campaign, writing for their magazine about USAS and Kukdong. In summer 2001 he was a member of USAS's Collegiate Apparel Research Initiative (CARI) in Mexico, assisting the Kukdong campaign. His responsibilities included documenting a "day in the life of a suspended Kukdong worker" for the anti-sweatshop website behindthelabel. org, and searching small towns finding the laid-off Kukdong workers whose addresses the union and the NGO did not have.

Since telling this story, **Yesenia Bonilla** has married. She now has a daughter, with whom she stays home full-time.

Elizabeth Brennan graduated in June 2001 from Northwestern University with a degree in journalism. There she campaigned to get the university to join the WRC. She travelled to Mexico in summer 2001 with USAS's CARI project and is now in Washington DC, establishing herself as a journalist.

Jess Champagne served on the USAS Coordinating Committee (1999), participated in the USAS–National Labor Committee 1999 delegation to El Salvador, and helped coordinate USAS's 2000 Collegiate Apparel Research Initiative in Indonesia. She has held editorial positions at several student, activist, and Jewish publications, including the *Yale Alternative*, the *Co-op America Quarterly*, and *New Voices*. Champagne graduated from Yale in 2001 with a degree in Anthropology.

HeeWon Taylor Khym graduated from Boston College, with a BS degree in Geology. There he was active with the pre-USAS movement. He spent some time in Guatemala working on economic development projects for women as well as educating and enrolling international observers within conflict zones in Chiapas, Mexico. In the summer of 2000, he participated in the AFL–CIO-sponsored Union Summer, working on UFCW (United Food and Commercial Workers) 1500's greengrocer campaign organizing Mexican immigrants. In the summer of 2001, he was chosen to be one of four interns in an AFL–CIO-sponsored internship program called International Union Summer, in which he was supervised by the Solidarity Center in Mexico and worked on the Kukdong campaign. He is now finishing his Masters in Public Administration program at

Columbia University's School of International Policy and Affairs and will be graduating in May 2002.

Micah Maidenburg spent two years as a student at Indiana University, where he was active in the campus anti-sweatshop group No Sweat! He then took time off to work as a union organizer for SEIU Local 880, a statewide home healthcare and daycare union in Illinois. His journalism has been published in the *Indiana Daily Student*, the *Marion* (Indiana) *Chronicle Tribune*, and the *Griot*, an independent newpaper that he co-edited. He is now back in school, at Oberlin College.

Chris McCallum is a recovering punk rocker who grew up in Bethlehem, Pennsylvania. He got politics when working with the *Student Underground*, a student-run, collectively organized alternative newspaper at Boston University, where he is a third-year journalism and environmental science major. McCallum has worked as an organizer for Hotel Employees and Restaurant Employees (HERE) Local 26 in Boston, and was part of the Summer 2000 Nike Truth Tour, a two-week cross-country mobile protest sponsored by UNITE! and USAS.

Molly McGrath, who became politically active as a Women's Studies major at the University of Wisconsin–Madison, has been involved in USAS almost since its inception. Her anti-sweatshop activism started in 1998 around the issue of the Collegiate Licensing Company's Code of Conduct. She participated in a 1999 sit-in protesting that Code's deficiencies, and joined a Press for Change anti-sweatshop delegation to Indonesia that summer. She served on the co-ordinating committee for eight months in 2000 and, on campus, helped plan another sit-in to pressure UW to join the Worker Rights Consortium. She graduated from UW in December 2001 and is now development director for the Madison, Wisconsin-based Progressive Media Project, which distributes op-eds to the commentary page of newspapers across the country.

A social studies major at Harvard University, **Benjamin McKean** has been an active member of USAS since September 1998, and helped found the Harvard Living Wage campaign later that year. In summer 2000 McKean was the International Union Summer Organizer in Guatemala with the AFL–CIO Center for International Labor Solidarity. His editorials about the Harvard Living Wage campaign, from which this book's essay is adapted, have appeared in the *Los Angeles Times* and the *Nation*.

As a student labor activist at Georgetown University, **Laura McSpedon** helped to start an anti-sweatshop campaign on campus in September of 1997, and became one of the founding members of USAS. In the summer of 1998, she participated in the first student delegation to investigate sweatshop conditions in Central America, and served on the USAS coordinating committee from July 1999 to January 2000. Since graduating in May 2000, she has worked at Jobs with Justice as the co-coordinator of the Student Labor Action Project (SLAP), a joint project of Jobs with Justice and the United States Student Association to provide resources and support to students defending workers' rights.

Saurav Sarkar graduated from Yale University with a BA in History in May 2000. As a junior, he was vice-chair of the Liberal Party of the Yale Political Union, and an editor of the *Yale Alternative*, where he co-authored an article that exposed a Salvadoran factory where Yale T-shirts were made under abusive labor conditions. During his senior year, he served as a head organizer for Yale's USAS chapter, helping to coordinate the nation's largest campus anti-sweatshop rally to date as well as a sixteen-day occupation of Beinecke Plaza, opposite the president's office. He has publicly debated Sam Brown, executive director of the Fair Labor Association. Since February 2001, Sarkar has worked for the National Labor Committee, where his main responsibility is Internet organizing.

At the University of North Carolina–Chapel Hill in 1997, **Marion Traub-Werner**, originally from Toronto, started a campaign exposing Nike's sweatshop abuses. After graduating in 1999, she moved to Central America to work directly with worker organizing in the apparel-for-export industry and to connect US solidarity groups, including students, to these efforts. She was an organizer for STITCH, a network of US labor organizers and community activists who support women's organizing in export industries in Central America. Now back in the United States, she is organizing for HERE.